# A Gross Breach
# of Justice

## The Flapper Election and After

# A Great Act of Justice

## The Flapper Election and After

*Nanette Sloane* (signature)

Editor: Nan Sloane

*'I hope all Members will realise that we are doing at last a great act of justice to the women of the country.'*

Ellen Wilkinson MP in the debate on the second reading
of the Representation of the People (Equal Franchise) Bill, 29 March 1928

**cfwd** Centre for Women and Democracy

**Centre for Women & Democracy**
2 Blenheim Terrace
Leeds LS2 9JG

www.cfwd.org.uk

Registered in England No 6106867

Design by: Barry Perks, yo-yo.uk.com

Printed in the UK by York Publishing Services Limited

Copyright © Centre for Women & Democracy 2009

First published December 2009
ISBN 978 0 9562637 0 4

We would especially like to thank the NASUWT for their support.

# NASUWT
The Teachers' Union

*The largest teachers' union in the UK*

Cover Images:

Main photo: Nancy Astor campaigning in 1923 Hulton Archive/Getty Images

Photos of (L to R) Margaret Bondfield, Jennie Lee, Megan Lloyd George and Ellen Wilkinson all © National Portrait Gallery, London

The Centre for Women & Democracy is an organisation independent of specific political or party interests. Views expressed in this publication are those of their authors, and do not necessarily represent the views of CFWD.

This publication may not be reproduced, in whole or in part, without the written permission of the Centre for Women & Democracy.

# Contents

| | |
|---|---|
| **Foreword** | 7 |
| by Chris Keates, General Secretary, NASUWT | |
| **Introduction** | 9 |
| by Nan Sloane, Director, Centre for Women & Democracy | |
| Some Parliamentary Firsts | 13 |
| **Part One: A Logical Necessity** | 15 |
| The Post-War Compromise | 16 |
| Women Elected 1918-1928 | 19 |
| Campaigning Women | 23 |
| Towards Universal Suffrage | 29 |
| Securing the Act | 37 |
| **Part Two: The Flapper Election** | 47 |
| The Election and the Women Who Won | 48 |
| The Women Who Lost | 58 |
| **Part Three: What Happened Next** | 65 |
| The Thirties | 66 |
| The 1945 Election | 73 |
| The Fifties | 80 |
| The Sixties | 85 |
| The Seventies | 88 |
| Breaking New Barriers, by Baroness Joyce Gould | 95 |
| The Eighties | 99 |
| Breaking Through on Merit by Rt Hon Baroness Betty Boothroyd OM | 108 |
| The Nineties | 112 |
| Women in Government | 118 |
| Women Cabinet Ministers 1919 – 2009 | 120 |

| | |
|---|---|
| The Twenty-First Century | 123 |
| Conservative Women | 130 |
| The Conservative Approach by Rt Hon Theresa May MP | 132 |
| Labour Women | 135 |
| Leading the Way by Maria Eagle MP | 137 |
| Liberal Democrat Women | 141 |
| Celebrating Progress: Encouraging More by Jo Swinson MP | 143 |
| Women of Other Parties and None | 147 |
| Women in Europe | 148 |
| A European Perspective by Linda McAvan MEP | 149 |
| UK Women Members of the European Parliament | 152 |
| Women in Devolved Institutions | 153 |
| Women in Politics in Wales by Baroness Anita Gale | 154 |
| 'Quietly Thrilling': Women and the Scottish Parliament by Fiona Mackay | 158 |
| Women in Politics in Northern Ireland by Bronagh Hinds | 162 |

## Part Four: The Next Level — 167

| | |
|---|---|
| Women Across the World | 168 |
| Moving Forward by Chris Keates | 171 |
| Are Votes at Sixteen the Answer? by Emily Beardsmore | 175 |
| Power Games: The Barriers for Ethnic Minority Women by zohra moosa | 178 |
| Making Politics Work: Changing the Way We Vote by Beatrice Barleon | 182 |
| A Brief Snip of Time by Boni Sones | 185 |
| And Finally ... | 188 |

**Sources and Acknowledgements** — 190
**Index** — 192

# Foreword

As the largest teacher' union in the UK the NASUWT is pleased and proud to be working in partnership with the Centre for Women and Democracy and to be sponsoring the 'Great Act of Justice'.

The 1929 Election, the first one where all women over the age of 21 were able to vote, was a momentous achievement, the result of a long struggle to secure equal franchise for all.

Yet, just over eighty years since the suffrage, women's representation in the British political system in Westminster stands at a mere one in five.

Across the UK there is appalling under representation of women in the political structures and decision making processes which shape our lives. Too few women make it to the top in public services or the private sector.

The trade union movement mirrors this under-representation. Trade union activism has been the stepping stone for many women to becoming involved in national and local politics. Emily Phipps, President of the National Federation of Women Teachers, a forerunner of the NASUWT, between 1915 and 1917, was an active suffragist and one of the first women parliamentary candidates. Many of today's women MPs were once active trade union members.

There can of course be no doubt that some progress has been made. There is a raft of equality legislation on the statute books which undoubtedly has been a key catalyst for change. However, structural inequalities in society and institutional sexism, continue to define women through the prism of biological stereotype as carers, nurturers, low grade administrators and organisers with so called 'soft skills' which are undervalued. Women in public life are still too often judged by age and appearance rather than ability.

The trade union movement has a powerful and influential role to play in changing attitudes. Much of the progress on equality issues has either been developed from within or campaigned for by trade unions, often by the women within the movement.

As a teachers' trade union the NASUWT also recognises the critical role of education. The structure of the curriculum, career choices and parental support are factors in transforming gender and cultural stereotypes. We all have a responsibility to put an end to the scandalous squandering of talent which results from discrimination against girls and women. Young women must be encouraged to realise their full potential and to be part of the decision making structures.

2018 will be the centenary of the Representation of the Peoples Act. 'One in five' must not be the statistic which marks that anniversary. Real change is needed to ensure that women are able to play their full and rightful part in the democratic process. Only then will the struggle started by the suffragette movement be at an end.

**Chris Keates**

*General Secretary*
*NASUWT*

# Introduction

*'... half the human race (is) not enough. It must be men and women together. To-night marks the final stage in the union of men and women working together for the re-generation of their country and for the re-generation of the world..'*

The Prime Minister, Stanley Baldwin, responding to the debate on the second reading of the Representation of the People (Equal Franchise) Act, 29 March, 1928

The first general election in which men and women in Britain could vote on the same terms was held on 30 May 1929. It was called the 'Flapper Election', after a word used to describe young women at the time, and it resulted in the election of a record fourteen women to the House of Commons (though they were still hugely outnumbered by the 601 men elected at the same time). There were nine Labour women, three Conservatives, one Liberal and one Independent. The oldest was sixty-eight, and the youngest twenty-four. They were all remarkable in one way or another. They were amongst the first into a field that had for centuries been dominated by men, and from which they had been excluded by a series of conscious and much-debated decisions. They had to contend with any number of practical difficulties as well as outright prejudice and discrimination, and they had to do it in a way which made them acceptable to the society around them. They did this in very individual ways, and although many of the problems and barriers they encountered were very different from those faced by their successors now, many – as we shall see – were depressingly similar.

The history of parliament across the centuries is not a history in which women have played the starring roles. The great turning-points in the development of British democracy were, until the twentieth century, almost entirely male events. As a result, the institution Nancy Astor entered as a lone female voice in 1919 had only male role models and reference points, and since the number of women MPs rose only very slowly over the succeeding decades, this did not change. As a result, the history of women in parliament is not well known – women whose contribution to the society in which we live as well as to the advance of women's representation have become lost as politicians in their own right and are largely remembered in terms of the men by whom they were surrounded, or are forgotten altogether.

Examples of this are not hard to find. Often the only thing people know about Nancy Astor (apart from her being the first woman to take her seat) are her exchanges with Winston Churchill, in which she is represented as a battle axe and in which she always came off worst. Ellen Wilkinson is rightly remembered for her support of the Jarrow Hunger Marchers, but the fact that, as Minister for Education, she brought in free school milk, raised the school leaving age and implemented the 1944 Education Act are forgotten. Very few women have ever achieved cabinet rank

– just one before the Second World War and a total, including Margaret Thatcher, of only twenty-seven since 1929 – so that the history of government in the twentieth century remains overwhelmingly male – a sort of jungle in which the big beasts crash noisily about. It is not a female environment, and women who enter it are expected to conform to it rather than change it.

Women were not particularly welcomed into the House of Commons – Nancy Astor observed that 'I had the privilege of being the first woman in the House of Commons, and sometimes I used to doubt whether it was a privilege. When I stood up and asked questions affecting women and children I used to be shouted at for five or ten minutes at a time[1] '. As women elected in 1997 could (and did) attest[2], not much changed in the succeeding decades, and although this is an aspect of politics less dwelt upon now, women politicians will still report problems privately.

Thus, although this book began as a commemoration of that single historic election of eighty years ago, and of the women who stood in it, it quickly became a celebration of women in parliament both before and since. There have been twenty-four general elections since women were first enfranchised (on a limited basis) in 1918, and in total only 5% of the MPs elected at them have been women. If 1997 – when the number of women MPs reached its all-time high to date – is excluded, the figure falls to a mere 3% for elections between 1918 and 1992. Women did not hold any of the major offices of state until Margaret Thatcher became prime minister in 1979; we had to wait until the twenty-first century for women to be appointed as either Foreign or Home Secretary, and there has still never been a female Chancellor of the Exchequer. Currently, only a fifth of our MPs are women, there are only two black women MPs, and there have never been any Asian women in the House of Commons. Disabled women have also been very poorly represented, and, to date, there has only been one openly gay woman elected. Some political parties have many more women MPs in their ranks than others; the House of Commons itself is still organised along lines more likely to suit men than women and retains a confrontational culture which views compromise, reflection and flexibility as weaknesses.

Today, we are still discussing how to improve the way our democracy works. Should people be allowed to vote at 16? Should we move to proportional representation? How can we re-establish trust in the political process and our politicians, and how can we encourage a wider range of people to get involved in politics and to stand for parliament? The Speaker of the House of Commons has established a Speaker's Conference to examine these and many other issues, and, at the time of writing, this Conference is still taking evidence. It will be interesting to see what will happen as a result of that process, and what new directions one of the oldest democracies in the world will now take.

[1] Speaking in the debate on the second reading of the 1928 Equal Franchise Bill
[2] Boni Sones with Margaret Moran and Joni Lovenduski, Women in Parliament: The New Suffragettes, London 2005

# The Flapper Election and After

When Stanley Baldwin, speaking in the debate on the Bill, said that 'half the human race was not enough', he was right. It is still not enough. But he over-estimated what the role of the 1928 Act in the history of progress towards 'the final stage of men and women working together' would be. He thought it was the end; we, with hindsight, know that it was only a staging post. Many women, in this country as in others, are still effectively excluded from participation, and business, trade unions, politics and many of the professions are still largely run by men, even where women are well-represented in them at lower levels. And the disproportionate under-representation of some specific groups of women is an issue which has come to prominence only in recent years, and which is likely to continue to be a matter for concern for some years to come.

The women who have contributed to this book represent a variety of views as to how those issues should be addressed. They all have differing views on how women's participation and representation can or should be advanced, and they range in age and experience from Baroness Betty Boothroyd, who was the first woman to be elected Speaker of the House of Commons, to Emily Beardsmore who, until recently was the chair of the British Youth Council. They come from a variety of political backgrounds, and they reflect a number of different perceptions and approaches. Their input lifts what might otherwise have been a rather dry account of a parliamentary debate and an election into a book which offers ways forwards as well as glances back.

For the twenty-first century may begin to change the way our politics look, feel and work. There are more women MPs, and their numbers will probably continue to increase. The current debate about the culture of politics will have to include consideration of the way in which the business of the House is conducted, and gradually the UK will inevitably begin to catch up with its nearest European neighbours in terms of the numbers of women in public life and the levels of diversity those women represent. Recovering some of women's parliamentary history – or at least remembering who the first women in the field were, and how they helped to create the world in which we live – has a part to play in that, and this book is an attempt to make an accessible and interesting contribution to that process.

We have used a number of sources and resources, and every reasonable effort has been made to ensure the accuracy of facts and figures and to acknowledge sources and copyright. Any errors or omissions remain our own, and we would be grateful if they could be pointed out to us.

We would also like to thank a number of people for their support, help and encouragement in this project – Laura Wigan for her painstaking research, York Publishing Services for their help, advice and flexibility in the face of delays, and all the contributors for their articles. But we would particularly like to thank Helen Russell at the National Union of Schoolmasters and Union of Women Teachers

(NASUWT) for her continued interest, Chris Keates, the General Secretary, for agreeing to write the Foreword, and the Union as a whole for their financial assistance, without which publication would not have been possible.

This book celebrates the women who, with courage, commitment, intelligence and perseverance, have got us to where we are today. Now we need to make sure that, when the centenary of universal suffrage is marked in 2029, both halves of the human race are equally represented in the places they first entered as pioneering voices.

**Nan Sloane**

*Director, Centre for Women & Democracy*
*Leeds*
*November 2009*

# The Flapper Election and After

# Some Parliamentary Firsts

Since women were first admitted to Parliament (as MPs in 1918, and as peers in 1958) there have been a number of significant firsts. Amongst them are:

|  |  |  |
|---|---|---|
| 1918 | First woman elected to House of Commons | Constance Markiewicz |
| 1919 | First woman to take her seat in the House | Nancy Astor |
| 1919 | First Conservative woman MP | Nancy Astor |
| 1921 | First Liberal woman MP | Margaret Wintringham |
| 1923 | First Labour women MPs | Margaret Bondfield<br>Susan Lawrence<br>Dorothy Jewson |
| 1924 | First woman minister | Margaret Bondfield |
| 1929 | First woman Cabinet minister | Margaret Bondfield |
| 1929 | First woman Privy Councillor | Margaret Bondfield |
| 1929 | First Independent woman MP | Eleanor Rathbone |
| 1958 | First woman life peer | Baroness Wooten of Abinger |
| 1963 | First woman hereditary peer | Baroness Strange of Knokin |
| 1975 | First woman Leader of the Conservative Party | Margaret Thatcher |
| 1979 | First woman Prime Minister | Margaret Thatcher |
| 1981 | First woman Leader of the House of Lords | Baroness (Janet) Young |
| 1987 | First black woman MP | Diane Abbott |
| 1990 | First Asian woman peer | Baroness (Shreela) Flather |
| 1992 | First openly gay woman MP | Angela Eagle |
| 1992 | First woman Speaker of the House of Commons | Betty Boothroyd |
| 1994 | First woman Leader of the Labour Party | Margaret Beckett |
| 1997 | First woman Leader of the House of Commons | Ann Taylor |
| 1997 | First black women peers | Baroness (Valerie) Amos<br>Baroness (Patricia) Scotland |
| 1998 | First woman Labour Chief Whip | Ann Taylor |
| 2003 | First black woman member of the Cabinet | Baroness (Valerie) Amos |
| 2006 | First woman Foreign Secretary | Margaret Beckett |
| 2007 | First woman Home Secretary | Jacqui Smith |
| 2008 | First black woman minister in the House of Commons | Dawn Butler |

# Part One:

# A Logical Necessity

*'... the Bill I am putting before the House is the logical outcome and the logical necessity of the various acts of politicians on both sides which have gradually led Parliament up to the position in which it is placed to-day.'*

The Home Secretary, Sir William Joynson-Hicks,
moving the second reading of the Bill, 29 March 1928

# The Post-War Compromise

In 1918, after a long fight lasting centuries rather than decades, some women finally won the right to vote in parliamentary elections, and all women over 21 became eligible for election as MPs.

The accepted version of women's political history – or, rather, of the history of the extension of the franchise – tends to cease at this point, albeit with a nod in the direction of the enfranchisement of women under thirty in 1928. But in fact the 1918 Act was just the start of a new phase in that history, and misconceptions and urban myths about both it and the later enfranchisement of young women still abound.

Prior to the First World War, there had been a wide-spread, vigorous and determined campaign for women's suffrage, yet despite everything, it had not been successful. Inevitably, the War changed the nature of the campaign, but it did not suppress it. Many women who had participated in it became engaged in a variety of other political, campaigning and caring activities, either in support of the war or in opposition to it, and in providing relief and support for refugees, wounded soldiers and widows and orphans. Throughout, however, a steady pressure to enfranchise women was maintained at one level or another, and, in 1916, the first Speaker's Conference was established to look at a variety of constitutional issues, of which one was the extension of the franchise.

The extension of it to women was not the only item on the agenda. The enfranchisement of men was, if anything, even higher on it; the electorate at the last election in 1910 had numbered fewer than eight million partly because of the total absence of women, but also because of the absence of the vast majority of men, most of whom could not meet the restrictive property qualifications.

There was general agreement that, after the horrors of the war, working class men should be given the vote; indeed, in the immediate aftermath of the war men as young as 19 were able to vote in some circumstances. But over the enfranchisement of women there was much more debate. The fact that if women were enfranchised on the same basis as men they would outnumber them on the electoral roll raised all sorts of fears in the minds of many people, and there was a great reluctance to create a situation in which the (male) political establishment could, in theory at least, be 'overwhelmed' by women. As a result the Speaker's Conference recommended that women should be allowed to vote, but that there should be an age limit. Various ages were canvassed, but finally thirty was settled upon.

The Representation of the People (Equal Franchise) Act of 1918 therefore enfranchised women over the age of thirty who were not subject to any legal incapacity, and who were married to (and resided with) men who met the property qualification, or who, if single, met it themselves. This enfranchised about six million women (still fewer than the entire male electorate had been in 1910), but left significant groups of women without a vote.

All men over the age of 21 were enfranchised (effectively without a property qualification), thus ending a campaign for manhood suffrage which had been waged for centuries, and which had often been seen as being in competition with, or having greater priority than, the campaign for women's suffrage.

In the minds of many people, women were being given the vote as a 'reward' for their hard work and sacrifice during the First World War. It was perhaps ironic, therefore, that all young women – many of whom had worked tirelessly in industry or in hospitals – were excluded, as were unmarried women of any age who did not meet the property qualification.

To complicate matters even further, the Parliament (Qualification of Women) Act of 1918 gave women over the age of 21 the right to become members of parliament, but did not restrict this right to women who could vote. As a result, women could – and did – become MPs without being able to vote in either their own or anyone else's election. This now seems bizarre, but at the time it appeared perfectly reasonable, since it simply brought the law for women into line with that for men, who had been eligible for election but not for the franchise for a considerable period.

The first general election to be held under this new franchise followed hard on the passing of the Act. The first challenge facing women was that of registering to vote, but although some reported considerable difficulty in registering, the majority of eligible women did get their names onto the electoral roll by the time the first post-war election took place on 14 December 1918.

There had been fears that there would be large numbers of women candidates – for whom women might vote en bloc – but, due to a mixture of a very tight electoral timetable, a lack of experience, and the view that women candidates could not win – these proved groundless, with only seventeen out of a total of 1,623 candidates being female.

Of those seventeen, only one – Constance, Countess Markiewicz was elected. The remaining 705 MPs (the House of Commons was larger at that time, because it still included the whole of Ireland) were men.

This was perhaps hardly surprising. The election was held in the immediate aftermath of an appalling war, and feelings were still running high. Many of the women candidates had been active in either the suffrage movement, or the peace movement, or both, and neither were popular with the public. In addition, there were instances such as that of Mary MacArthur, who, although known to the public under her maiden name, had to appear on the ballot paper under her married name. Despite this, a number of the women candidates did well, collecting respectable percentages of the vote and fighting active and effective campaigns.

Constance Markiewicz had been elected as a Sinn Fein MP and therefore never took her seat as a matter of principle (quite apart from the fact that she was in Holloway Gaol at the time of her election). Nancy, Viscountess Astor – elected at a by-election in 1919 – was the first and the only woman actually in parliament until 1921, when she was joined by Margaret Wintringham for the Liberals, and she remained the sole woman in the Conservative parliamentary party until 1923, when Katharine Stewart-Murray (the Duchess of Atholl) and Mabel Philipson were elected.

The first Labour women – Margaret Bondfield, Susan Lawrence and Dorothy Jewson – were also elected in 1923, as was the second Liberal MP, Vera, Lady Terrington.

Both Nancy Astor and Margaret Wintringham won their seats at by-elections, and both succeeded their husbands. This pattern – of wives succeeding to husbands' seats – was repeated more than once in the ensuing decade. Of the eleven women who sat as MPs between 1918 and 1929, four 'inherited' their seats from their husbands (Nancy Astor, Margaret Wintringham, Mabel Philipson and the Countess of Iveagh). In addition, Ruth Dalton – who, jointly with Margo Macdonald in the 1970s holds the record (92 days) for the shortest time in parliament – was elected for a safe seat at a by-election to 'keep it warm' for her husband, and Hilda Runciman, who won a safe seat for the Liberals, passed it on to her husband and contested (and lost) a more marginal seat nearby.

It is also striking to the modern eye that five of the twelve women elected in these years had titles, and were known by them during their political lifetimes. This is now unusual, but at the time there were far more titles of one kind or another – particularly military – in the Commons, although even then the presence of a duchess was remarkable.

Many of the things that had so worried opponents of female suffrage before and during the War did not materialise. Women did not vote as a single bloc, but distributed their votes between existing parties. There was a short-lived Women's Party (set up by the Women's Social & Political Union, which had spearheaded the suffragette element of the suffrage campaign), and Nancy Astor made a similar suggestion during the nineteen-twenties, but neither took off. Women were interested – or not interested – in politics to much the same degree as their husbands, and their enfranchisement did not in and of itself lead to any sudden political upheavals.

However, the addition of six million women to the electoral register, combined with the addition of over seven million men, did produce or accelerate a number of changes, with the Labour Party taking an increasingly significant proportion of the votes, the Liberal Party beginning its long electoral decline, and the election of the first women MPs. Meanwhile, the campaign to enfranchise all women continued.

# Women Elected 1918 - 1928

Between the partial enfranchisement of 1918 and universal suffrage in 1929, a grand total of 13 women were elected to parliament. There were general elections in 1918, 1922, 1923 and 1924, and the list below shows who the successful women were, and at which elections they were successful.

Only 12 of these women were actually sworn in; Constance Markievicz refused to take her seat as a matter of principle and never served as an MP. The first woman to take her seat, therefore, was Nancy Astor in 1919.

|  | Constituency | Elections | Party |
|---|---|---|---|
| Constance, Countess Markievicz | Dublin St Patrick's | 1918 | Sinn Féin |
| Nancy, Viscountess Astor | Plymouth Sutton | 1919 (by-election) | Con |
| Margaret Wintringham | Louth | 1921 (by-election), 1923 | Lib |
| Katharine Stewart-Murray, Duchess of Atholl | Perth & Kinross | 1923, 1924 | Con |
| Margaret Bondfield | Northampton/Wallsend | 1923, 1926 | Lab |
| Dorothy Jewson | Norwich | 1923 | Lab |
| Susan Lawrence | East Ham North | 1923, 1926 | Lab |
| Mabel Philipson | Berwick-upon-Tweed | 1923, 1924 | Con |
| Vera, Lady Terrington | Wycombe | 1923 | Lib |
| Ellen Wilkinson | Middlesbrough East | 1924 | Lab |
| Gwendolen Guinness, Countess of Iveagh | Southend-on-Sea | 1927 (by-election) | Con |
| Hilda Runciman | St Ives | 1928 (by-election) | Lib |
| Ruth Dalton | Bishop Auckland | 1929 (by-election) | Lab |

# A Great Act of Justice

# Constance Markiewicz

The first woman to be elected to parliament was born in London 1868. She had a conventional upbringing in a liberal family environment, and studied art in both London, where she was active in the suffrage movement, and Paris, where she met, and in 1900 married, Count Casimir Markiewicz.

The couple returned to Ireland, where Constance gave birth to her only child, Maeve, and became increasingly actively involved with Irish nationalism. Through this she met many leading independence activists, including the future leaders of the Easter Rising. At the same time, she maintained her interest in women's suffrage, being part of a successful campaign to prevent the election of Winston Churchill (who thought politics unsuitable for women) in Manchester in 1908.

Her views on Ireland, however, became steadily more militant, and in 1911 she was jailed following an address to an Irish Republican Brotherhood rally in Dublin. In 1913 she joined the Irish Citizen Army, and in the 1916 Rising served as the Army's second in command at St Stephen's Green. She was arrested, kept in solitary confinement in Kilmainham Jail, and sentenced to death. As the executions of the other rebels began her sentence was commuted to life imprisonment – she is reported to have said 'I wish you had the decency to shoot me'.

In 1917 she was released as part of an amnesty, but in 1918 she was back in prison for anti-conscription activities. In December 1918, whilst still a prisoner, she stood for election to the Westminster Parliament as a Sinn Fein candidate for the Dublin St Patrick constituency and was elected, although, along with other Republicans, she refused (even after her release) to take her seat.

At the same time, she became the first woman to be elected to the First Dail Éireann, set up in advance of actual independence, and in which she served as Minister of Labour between 1919 and 1922. She was again elected to the Dail in 1921, and – with a short interval, and despite differences with the new nationalist leadership – remained a member until her death (aged 59) in 1927.

# Nancy, Viscountess Astor

Born in Virginia in 1879, Nancy Astor was one of the more colourful politicians of her time. She was married to Waldorf Astor, who became a Conservative MP in 1910, but had little interest in politics herself. In 1919, however, Waldorf became Viscount Astor and had to resign his seat. Nancy dutifully stood in the subsequent by-election and won, going on to represent Plymouth Sutton until 1945.

Once she had been elected she accepted with enthusiasm the responsibility of being the first – and for a time the only – woman in parliament, and she quickly built working relationships with key women's organizations. Women all over the country regarded her as 'their' MP, and she had to respond to a vast postbag on a huge variety of subjects.

She was also very keen to get more women into parliament and strongly supported the extension of the franchise. She was perfectly prepared to work across party lines on specific projects, and often found it difficult to fit in with the political structures and disciplines within which she was required to work.

Her personal politics were generally conservative, occasionally naïve, and sometimes very idiosyncratic. Her greatest legislative achievement was the 1923 Act introducing a legal minimum age (18) for the sale of alcohol.

She supported widow's pensions, equal employment and measures to reduce maternal mortality rates, as well as the Association for Moral and Social Hygiene which campaigned to equalise moral standards for both men and women. She also favoured reform of the House of Lords.

Ironically, as more women entered parliament, Nancy Astor became more isolated, although she remained famous for her house parties at Cliveden, her strange mix of friends (ranging from George Bernard Shaw to the German ambassador) and her wit, but her eclectic mix of opinions and her unpredictability meant that her party came to regard her as a liability rather than an asset. Her parliamentary career came to an end in 1945, when she (unwillingly) stood down, and she died in 1964.

# A Great Act of Justice

# Margaret Wintringham

Margaret Wintringham was born in 1879 in Keighley in West Yorkshire, and was headteacher of a school in Grimsby. She married Thomas Wintringham, a timber merchant, in 1903.

She was involved in a range of social and political movements, from temperance to the Townswomen's Guild, and including the National Union of Societies for Equal Citizenship and the Liberal Party.

In 1920, when Thomas was elected as the MP for Louth, the couple moved to the town, where Margaret's wide range of activities continued. In 1925 and 1926, she was President of the Women's National Liberal Federation, and in 1927, she was one of only two women to be elected onto the national executive of the Liberal Federation.

When Thomas Wintringham died in 1921, Margaret stood in the subsequent by-election. With support from prominent political women from all over the country, and, despite the opposition of the local press and a strong campaign against her, she won the seat.

She was thus the first Liberal woman MP, and also the first British-born woman to be elected.

In parliament, Margaret worked across party lines with Nancy Astor on a number of issues, and 1921 they set up the Consultative Committee of Women's Organizations. She was interested in educational reform, as well reform of the House of Lords, and pay and conditions for both male and female agricultural workers.

Although re-elected in 1922 and 1923, Margaret Wintringham lost her seat in the general election of 1924, and despite attempts to return to parliament in 1929 and 1935 her career in the Commons was over. She remained active, however, and continued to campaign on issues which interested her, sitting as a member of Royal Commissions and working with the Women's Land Army during the Second World War. She died in 1955.

# Campaigning Women

As soon as women were eligible to be Members of Parliament, it became evident that those who stood would need support and training in running their campaigns. Some had experience of the suffrage campaign, and some simply inherited election machines from their predecessors (not infrequently, in these early years, their husbands). Others had to work it out as they went along. As a result, organizations such as the National Union of Societies for Equal Citizenship (the successor body to the National Union of Suffrage Societies) began to produce advice for women who now had to embark upon new forms of campaigning.

In 1921, the NUSEC produced a pamphlet entitled *'Notes on Election Work: for the use of women candidates and their workers'*. A short and practical pamphlet of a mere twenty-four pages, it had a foreword by Nancy Astor, a considerable amount of legal information, and plenty of excellent advice, some of which would be of as much benefit to candidates in the early twenty-first century as it was when it was published.

At the time of publication, Nancy Astor was still the only woman MP, and had been in parliament for a little over a year. Her introduction was of admirable brevity, and is worth quoting almost in full.

> *'I very much hope that the useful information and the good advice collected here will encourage many other women to come forward as candidates, and will help them to be successful at the polls.*
>
> *'I should like to emphasise as strongly as I can that no amount of organization or canvassing will get a woman candidate into parliament. For her, at any rate, there must be endless hard work in her constituency, until she has made friends with her constituents, and until they have grown to respect her work and her personality.*
>
> *'It is not an easy job for a woman to stand for Parliament, and it is not an easy job when one gets there; but the work waiting to be done is almost unlimited, and the need for the help of women is great and urgent.'*

The body of the pamphlet then began with the dry legal requirements, with which many potential women candidates would have been wholly unacquainted. That done, the authors turned to the matter of the campaign itself, beginning with a section called 'Choice of Candidate'. One observation made there remains true today.

> *'There can be no doubt that at present women belonging to the three great political parties have a much better chance of election than independent candidates.*

> 'It is therefore of the greatest importance that women belonging to the various parties should take an active part in the work of their organization ... '

The section entitled 'Personal Qualities' outlined the attributes of a good woman candidate:

> '(She) should be a good "feminist", e.g. (sic) she should thoroughly understand questions relating to the lives of women, whether as wives and mothers or as producers and workers, and she should firmly believe in the equality of status, liberty and opportunity between men and women.'

> 'She should have had some experience of local government or other forms of conspicuous public work, if possible in the constituency in which she is standing.'

Women candidates were also urged to develop and maintain a real interest in and knowledge of wider political questions, so that men (who still formed the majority of the electorate) as well as women 'shall be able to look at her as their representative.' The next paragraph, quoted here in full, contains advice which every politician would do well to heed.

> 'A good memory for names and faces, genial manners, a faculty for humorous repartee, the knack of answering letters promptly and giving a friendly and informal twist even to business communications – these things may, though they should not, carry a candidate farther than learning and sound political knowledge.'

Women were advised to cultivate a good speaking manner, since this would help them to overcome the prejudice they would undoubtedly encounter. 'In these days of large constituencies[1]' the pamphlet advised 'public appearances as a speaker are almost her only opportunities of making her personality known to the rank and file of the electorate.'

Today there is much interest in and comment on women politicians' clothes and appearance, but the 1921 pamphlet contains nothing at all about how the woman candidate should dress. The authors may have hoped that the trivial matter of fashion would never become an issue, but, if so, they were sadly mistaken; within three years Lady Terrington would be suing the Daily Express for a story it ran during her election campaign under the headline 'Aim if Elected – Furs and Pearls'. The Daily Express won, partly because Lady Terrington had actually said some of the things attributed to her, and partly because the jury decided that the dress of women MPs was a matter of public interest – an interest which, over eighty years later, seems to have mounted almost to an obsession.

---

[1] In 1928 the average size of a county constituency was 30,000; after the Act it climbed to 37,500. At the next general election it will stand at 70,000

# The Flapper Election and After

The pamphlet addressed the problems and expenses of nursing a constituency, and of working with, or developing, local organizational capacity at some length. Nursing a constituency was thought to be harder for a woman than for a man because of the 'steady period of solid spadework for months or even years beforehand' that was necessary. It was also likely to be an expensive process. The cost (excluding election expenses) of running a campaign in a 'cheap' constituency was estimated at between £300 and £500 a year.[2] To fund this, the woman candidate was advised to convene a meeting of the constituency party's committee and to:

> '... lay the needs of the work frankly before them and state what she herself can afford to pay. They should then elect a finance committee to raise a guarantee fund to meet the difference.'

Much of the booklet was devoted to the campaign and its organization. Then, as now, organization on the ground might not match up to expectations; the authors warned that:

> 'In many constituencies the candidate will find that she will have to create, practically from the beginning, the machine by which the election must be prepared for and won.... even when she is the nominee of a Party. She will perhaps be led to believe that the Party machine is a "going concern" only to find that it exists merely in skeleton, or is so rusty that it breaks down when tested.'

There follows much excellent advice, a good deal of it almost indistinguishable from what would be given now, on how to organise canvassing, how to allocate work, and the importance of training and nurturing volunteers. Later on, in the section devoted to running a committee room, very specific advice is given about keeping records, following up queries and requests from canvassing, making sure that people were properly prepared for the jobs they were asked to do, and that their contribution to them was recognised. On the committee room itself the writers observed that:

> 'Committee rooms run by women are as a rule not unnaturally neater and tidier than those run by men. There must be no confusion and no fuss, no waste of time, loitering about and talking.'

In dealing with volunteers, a degree of forbearance was also required – 'It ought to be needless to say that questions and enquiries, however stupid, must be attended to with the same infinite patience and politeness which should characterise the whole campaign.'

The choice of an election agent was crucial, the main thing being to find one who understood 'the intricacies of the law'. Such an individual was likely to be a man, and the pamphlet remarks that:

---

[2] £300 is equal to about £6,300 nowadays, and £500 to £10,600.

> 'Some election agents are very conservative in their methods, whatever they may be in their politics, and women accustomed to the bolder methods of the suffrage campaign may chafe against the too frequent use of that objectionable word "impossible"'.

Candidates were advised to build up a detailed knowledge of the constituency, and to keep a book in which information was recorded. One of the appendices gives a list of areas of research for this record; this includes details about key local people, other candidates, the sitting MP (his views, activities, and sayings), facts about all the towns and villages, the relevant industries and factories, details of the secretaries of local organizations, (particularly women's organizations), where to get maps, good places for public meetings and committee rooms, details of the local papers and their editors, lists of possible helpers, information about local transport, lists of restaurants, hotels, lodging houses, charwomen, livery stables, bill posters and gas and water companies, when early closing day was, where the polling stations were and the name and address of the returning officer. This book would need continual updating, and was an essential part of the candidate's campaign.

Other key elements included canvassing, the election address (which should be 'clear and as short as possible', and in which the candidate, whilst taking advice, should not 'be persuaded into allowing others to improve away any trace of her own personality'), and public meetings.

Nowadays, politicians tend to hark back to a golden age when public meetings were filled with interested electors seeking enlightenment, but in 1921 there was already a view that their importance could be over-estimated. 'They are apt', said the authors, 'to be attended mainly by those already interested', and could not be a substitute for 'steady, conscientious canvassing'. But they could be used to inspire supporters to greater efforts, or to get press coverage for the campaign, and should therefore be planned and delivered with meticulous attention to detail.

To begin with, the chair should, if possible, be a man, and there should be a very small number of (brief) speeches. There should be proper efforts made to build an audience, and there should be good and welcoming stewarding arrangements. The hall itself should be made as attractive as possible 'as in the old suffragette days'. Every effort should be made to get the local reporters to attend, and the gist of the candidate's speech should be typed up ready to distribute.

But the main part of the meeting should be devoted to questions, and clearly the candidate would be judged to a great degree on how she handled them. But it was also possible to plan for what some of those questions might be.

> 'Questions should be freely encouraged. Many women who are really interested are still afraid to lift up their voices in public and if provided with slips of paper by the stewards will send up excellent and helpful questions.'

Whether the questions were planted or not, the answers to them should always be 'short and to the point'. The candidate 'should not pretend to be omniscient; if a question is beyond her powers she should frankly say so and promise to look into the matter'. The pamphlet also recognised the possibility that the candidate might not actually have an opinion on every issue, and advises:

> *'If, on certain matters not prominently before the country at that special election she has not yet made up her mind, she should not be afraid to say so, and should state that should she be elected she will welcome any help her constituents may give her in forming her opinion.'*

Public meetings are still in use today, but other suggested ways of attracting attention are rather less likely to find favour now.

> *'When the election is actually in progress, the local picture theatre may sometimes be induced to display a film without charge, e.g., of the candidate writing a letter, or shaking hands with the oldest elector, or playing with her children. It is a good plan to get the candidate's name introduced into some short, jingling rhyme, sung to a popular tune, which can be taught to the school children.'*

The suggestion that the candidate should be seen playing with her children is not quite as twee as it might seem; in 1922 the seasoned suffrage campaigner Ray Strachey was forced to issue a leaflet stating:

> *'PLEASE NOTE: Mrs Oliver Strachey is NOT a Bolshevist, an Atheist or a Communist. Her husband was NOT a Conscientious Objector and her children are NOT neglected.'* [3]

To help candidates (and inexperienced agents) to stay on the right side of election expenses law, a sample set of expenses was given; it is presumed to be for an average-sized constituency of 29,959 electors and totals £627.0.8 (£13,299 at today's values). [4]

Some of the society women who stood would have been able to fund themselves, but for others the sheer scale of the expense must have been daunting. Many women recognised this at the time, and it was frequently cited as one of the reasons why there were so few women candidates overall. Even with party support, women were unlikely to be able to afford a campaign unless they either had personal or

---

[3] Quoted by Cheryl Law in Suffrage & Power: The Women's Movement 1918-1928, p 152

[4] The Electoral Commission's report on the 2005 General Election gave the average spend per constituency as just under £4,000 (though much more in marginal constituencies or by winning candidates), and the average limit per constituency as about £12,000. The cost of campaigning at local level actually seems to have gone down rather than up, and the amounts candidates and constituencies were expected to raise were well in excess of what present-day local parties and candidates either could or (in many cases) would consider raising.

family wealth, or were supported by a trade union, the women's organizations or other interested groups or individuals. The pamphlet's rather blithe assumption that a meeting with the constituency committee would resolve the financial issue may have been more wishful thinking than reality, as indeed it would be today.

Finally, the pamphlet gave a list of countries which already had women in their parliaments. These were Austria, some of the Canadian states, the Crimea (now part of the Ukraine), Czecho Slovakia (now two countries), Denmark, Estonia, Finland, Germany, Hungary, Lettonia (now Latvia), Lithuania, the Jewish National Assembly of Palestine, Luxembourg, the Netherlands, Poland and Rhodesia (now Zimbabwe).

Armed with good advice from sources such as NUSEC, supported (at least notionally) by political parties and often by women's organizations, women candidates during the nineteen twenties began to develop their expertise in a new field.

But there were other campaigns besides elections to be won – millions of women in 1921 had the vote, but millions of others did not, and the battle for universal suffrage still remained to be won.

# Towards Universal Suffrage

For some people, the fight for women's suffrage was now effectively over, and although it was generally recognised that there was some mopping up to do, it was not anticipated that this would happen for many years, if not decades. But for many women and women's organizations, the work was still far from complete. Equalization of voting rights remained an objective still to be won, and whilst campaigning never reached either the heights or the ferocity of the pre-war years, it never actually ceased, either.

During the 1920s, there were many changes to women's lives. The 1919 Sex Disqualification (Removal) Act made it possible for women to enter professions that had previously been closed to them, and gradually a succession of 'firsts' occurred. The first women magistrates were appointed in that year, and increasing numbers of women were elected to local boards and councils. In 1921 Victoria Drummond became the first woman member of the Institute of Marine Engineers. In 1922, Helena Normanton became the first woman barrister, and Carrie Morrison became the first woman solicitor. In the same decade Aileen Cust became the first female vet and Irene Barclay the first female chartered surveyor.

Thus by 1928 women were represented in many new professions; they could (as MPs) make the law and as solicitors and barristers work in it, but millions of them could still not vote to elect the legislators who would make it.

There were also significant improvements to women's lives in other ways, at least in part due to the presence of a tiny number of women in parliament. In 1921, an allowance for wives was added to the unemployment benefit, and the following year women secured equal inheritance rights with their husbands. In 1923, the Matrimonial Causes Act gave women the right to petition for divorce on the grounds of adultery on the part of the husband and two years later women won the right to an equal claim with men over the custody of children.

These advances were accompanied, however, by other, more retrograde, steps. During the War, women had increasingly entered jobs in both the public and private sectors; now they were being forced back out of them, or, if permitted to remain, forced to accept pay and conditions which were far from satisfactory. In addition, professions and organizations including local government, teaching, the civil service and the BBC joined others in banning the employment of married women, and the practice of women giving up work when they got married became entrenched, if not in law, at least in custom and practice from this time on. Together with the campaign for equal pay, it was a major issue for working women for decades, with echoes of it persisting even today.

Despite this, a woman born in 1900 into a world in which women's rights were few and restricted, in which the vast majority of professions were closed to her and in which she had no political rights, reached her late twenties with far greater protection under the law, the ability to earn her own living in new ways (provided, increasingly, that she remained unmarried and, in many cases, was prepared to accept a lower rate of pay), and the right to become an MP if she could, but without the right to vote. The War had also resulted in an unusually large number of unmarried and widowed women who had to earn their own living, but who did not own property and were therefore disenfranchised. As the decade wore on these anomalies became both more obvious and less acceptable.

For the political parties, the full enfranchisement of women also remained an issue, as did how to integrate them satisfactorily into the existing political system once they had entered it. The twenties marked the development of increasingly partisan women's political organizations, with cross-party working being discouraged in some cases and actively undermined or prohibited in others. The cost of election campaigns, and the electorate's disinclination to vote for independent or minority party candidates, meant that women who wished to be parliamentary candidates were forced to make party political choices in order to have even the chance of success.

But women were not expected to change or influence the male party structures into which they were now invited, and many women, particularly those who had been involved in the much more flexible suffrage organizations, found them rigid and unwelcoming. Parties were not generally inclined to give women equal membership rights, and recruited them more because they needed women's support at elections than because they wanted the experience and expertise women could bring. The ability of women members to influence and change political parties has remained problematic ever since.

For the electorate, however, political parties are a convenient way of making political decisions, and in the whole history of women's representation in parliament only one independent woman has ever been elected – Eleanor Rathbone between 1929 and 1945 for the Combined English Universities constituency (although Bernadette Devlin (McAliskey) was elected in 1969 in Mid-Ulster on an Independent Unity ticket).

Despite their reservations, political parties were quick to see that the addition of over eleven million new voters to the register in 1918 would necessarily mean a change to many aspects of political life, and much of their effort during the ensuing years was directed towards controlling, containing and minimising that change. The new women on the register were out-numbered by the new men, and women still made up less than a third of the electorate. The needs of post-war reconstruction, and, as the twenties wore on, the worsening economic situation, led to women's issues and political advance being increasingly marginalised, and women themselves came under considerable pressure to be 'mainstream' in their politics rather than feminised or feminist. Thus, from the outset, women politicians began to try to blend in with their male counterparts, and to behave and dress in ways which would not differentiate them from the male norm. This is a pressure from which women in politics still suffer, and which has yet to be resolved.

The first years of the decade saw a flurry of general elections, in none of which the equalisation of the franchise played any important role – in most cases it failed to feature even as an aside in party programmes and manifestoes. But women did appear – even if only in small numbers – as candidates, with varying degrees of success.

The general election which took place on 15 November 1922 was the result of the withdrawal of the Conservatives from the post-war coalition government. Two women MPs – the Conservative Nancy Astor and Liberal Margaret Wintringham – were defending their seats, and 31 other women also stood. All bar two of them were fielded by established political parties, but, in the event, only Nancy Astor and Margaret Wintringham, were elected.

A year later Stanley Baldwin called an election for 6 December over the issues of trade protection and unemployment. The number of women candidates now increased to 34, with the Labour Party fielding markedly more than previously. Since Labour did well in the election, Labour women did well also, and three – Margaret Bondfield, Susan Lawrence and Dorothy Jewson were elected, together with a second Liberal (Vera, Lady Terrington), and two more Conservatives – Katharine Stewart-Murray, Duchess of Atholl, and Mabel Philipson. This brought the total number of women MPs up to eight.

This success, however, was short-lived, since the Labour government which, at the beginning of 1924 had taken power with Baldwin's support, fell from office, causing yet another election on 29 October of that year. Labour's prospects were not good to begin with, but the publication of forged 'evidence' that the party was secretly plotting violent revolution sealed its fate. All three Labour women lost their seats, as did Margaret Wintringham and Lady Terrington. The only new woman to enter parliament was Ellen Wilkinson, who won Middlesbrough for Labour, and the number of women MPs was reduced to four. The number of women candidates had risen to 39.

In the meantime, the campaign to equalise the franchise had continued. In 1920 a Labour MP, Thomas Grundy, introduced a private member's bill to achieve equal voting rights. This bill passed its second reading, but a combination of determination on the part of the government not to allow it to become law, inexperience on the part of recently-elected Labour MPs, and the fact that Nancy Astor was at this stage the lone female voice in the House, meant that the bill ran out of time,.

This pattern of pressure from outside parliament, followed by a private member's bill which ran out of time, was repeated in 1923 when Isaac Foot's franchise bill also fell by the wayside. By this stage women in almost all the other countries of the British Empire already had an equal franchise, leaving the 'mother country' as the only one where a large section of the female population was deemed incapable of political participation. Moves were made to increase both the strength and the visibility of the campaign, and women once again came together across political and other divides to promote it.

The election in 1923 – albeit with Conservative support – of a minority Labour government raised new hopes. The Labour Party had had policy favouring an equal franchise for some years, and a number of individuals in it were personally committed to equalisation. However, this first Labour government was always fragile, and Ramsay Macdonald did not see constitutional reform as one of its priorities. The third private member's bill of the decade – introduced by William Adamson – got through to the committee stage but encountered the usual delaying tactics from its opponents. This was the first suffrage debate in which women MPs were involved on both sides of the argument, with the Duchess of Atholl working on behalf of the government to hold the bill up, not least on the grounds that it would also enfranchise the remnant of men who could not vote. Nancy Astor, on the other hand, though a member of the same party, supported the bill, together with the Labour and Liberal women.

In the event, the bill went the way of all the rest, gaining majorities at all the parliamentary stages it passed through, but unable to reach the end of its course. The 1924 General Election arrived with women's electoral position unchanged.

There did seem, however, to be some change in the Conservative Party's attitude to the question. Stanley Baldwin published a statement in the newspapers which said that the Conservative Party was in favour of equal political rights, and that, if it was elected, it would call another Speaker's Conference to examine the position. This was a pledge which would come back to haunt him, but at the time, taken together with the other two parties' longer standing commitments, it seemed to offer some hope, which even the rather dismal fortunes of women candidates at the polls could not dampen.

The failure of the Speaker's Conference to appear in the subsequent King's Speech was discouraging, however, and in February 1925 the old round of private member's bills was resumed by the Labour MP William Whiteley. The Home Secretary rejected it on a number of grounds, one of which was that a Speaker's Conference had been pledged, though it now seemed that this would take place in 1926 rather than 1925.

As the months wore on without any sign of progress, the women's organizations outside parliament began to increase the level of campaigning, with some women advocating a resumption of pre-war direct action. Baldwin compounded the problem by refusing to meet representatives of the campaign to discuss the situation, and throughout 1925 and 1926 activity increased. Baldwin finally did meet a delegation in early 1927 and indicated that he would be making a statement on the franchise shortly. The general expectation was that this would relate to the Conference, and there was therefore astonishment on all sides at the eventual announcement that a bill to equalise the voting age at 21 would be introduced in the next session of parliament.

Given their experience of previous such promises, women took nothing for granted and continued to campaign and to bring pressure to bear on both individual MPs and the government to make sure that they kept Baldwin's promise. Their scepticism seemed well-founded when no bill appeared in the King's Speech at the opening of parliament in February 1928. Possibly in response to the level of outrage expressed, Baldwin announced in the House on that same evening that a franchise bill would nevertheless be introduced in that session, and thus the Representation of the People (Equal Franchise) Bill finally made its appearance on 13 March 1928.

Now the only thing that remained was to make sure that the bill was passed.

# Susan Lawrence

'Our Susan', as she was known, was born in 1871, the daughter of a solicitor. She was educated at Newnham College, Cambridge before becoming a school manager and organiser for the National Federation of Women Workers.

In 1900 she was elected to the London School Board, and in 1910 she was elected as a Conservative member of the London County Council. Two years later she resigned from the party over rates of pay for school cleaners. As a result she became involved in working class women's organizations and then the Labour Party.

In 1913, she became a Labour member of Poplar Council, and after the First World War worked on reconstruction and issues facing women workers. In 1918 she was elected to the Labour Party's National Executive Committee as part of the new women's section.

In 1919 Labour-controlled Poplar Council began to take on the government by refusing to set a rate which would effectively have taxed the poor. As this dispute was developing, Susan stood unsuccessfully in a parliamentary by-election in Camberwell North West. In 1921, together with other Poplar councillors, she served five weeks in prison.

In 1923, she was elected as the MP for East Ham, becoming one of the first three Labour women MPs, but lost her seat in the disastrous 1924 General Election.

Eighteen months later the new Conservative MP died; Susan Lawrence was re-elected in the ensuing by-election. She served as a Parliamentary Secretary in the 1929 Labour Government, and in 1930, she became the first woman to chair the Labour Party Conference.

In 1931 she refused to join Ramsey MacDonald's National Government and lost her seat at the General Election of that year.

In 1935, she stood in Stockton-on-Tees but lost to Harold Macmillan. She remained politically active, both during and after the War, and died in 1947.

# Dame Katharine Stewart-Murray, Duchess of Atholl

Katharine Stewart-Murray was born in 1874, and trained at the Royal College of Music as a pianist. However, she never played professionally and in 1899 she married the heir to the duchy of Atholl and became active in Scottish charity and political work.

In 1908 she became president of the Perthshire Unionist Women's Association, and in 1910 her husband became the MP for Perthshire West. Katharine remained increasingly and extensively involved in Scottish public life, and in 1918 she became one of the first women to be created a Dame in her own right; by then her husband had inherited the dukedom and left the Commons.

In 1923 she was elected as the MP for Perth & Kinross, becoming the first Scottish woman in the House of Commons. She pursued an idiosyncratic political course, opposing many measures for women's equality and the raising of the school-leaving age, but successfully securing legislation to improve benefits for Scottish unmarried mothers.

She was also not averse to working across party lines on issues that concerned her, and collaborated with both Eleanor Rathbone and Ellen Wilkinson to campaign against female circumcision.

Her major dispute with her party came over the Spanish Civil War, in which she fiercely opposed Franco. She set up an all-party committee to rescue refugee children from the war, and became increasingly infuriated by the government's failure to enforce the non-intervention pact. She became known as the Red Duchess, but in 1938 she lost the party whip and then resigned her seat. In the by-election which followed she stood as an Independent with support from the left, but when she was narrowly defeated. her parliamentary career came to an end.

After the War, she concentrated on opposing communism in Europe. In 1945 she founded the British League for European Freedom, becoming as unpopular with the left as she had been with the right earlier. She died in 1960.

# Gwendolen Guinness, Countess of Iveagh

Born the Honourable Gwendolen Onslow in London in 1881, the Countess of Iveagh grew up in wealthy circumstances, and in 1903 married Rupert Guinness, who, between 1912 and 1927 was MP for Southend-on-Sea.

Gwendolen was herself politically active, working in all of her husband's election campaigns and, during the First World War, organising the provision of relief for British prisoners of war. In 1920, in recognition of this work, she was awarded the CBE.

After the enfranchisement of many women in 1918, the Conservative Party made great (and successful) efforts to recruit women to support it, and Gwendolen was at the forefront of these campaigns, chairing the Women's Advisory Committee between 1925 and 1933. In 1930 she chaired the National Union of Conservative and Unionist Associations.

In 1927, Rupert became the Earl of Iveagh and thus a member of the House of Lords. Gwendolen stood in the by-election which followed and was elected. She was throughout her parliamentary career a party loyalist, and remained on the back benches. The only speech she made between the by-election and her re-election in 1929 was during the Equal Franchise Bill debate in 1928, when, amongst other things, she observed that women of all parties found it very difficult to get winnable seats.

In 1935 she retired from parliament, handing her seat on to her son-in-law, Sir Henry Channon. However, she remained active, working with the Overseas Training School (preparing young women for emigration to the colonies), as well as maintaining interests in agricultural matters.

The family's parliamentary connection with Southend continued long after her retirement. Her son-in-law remained its MP until his death in 1958, and was then succeeded by his son, Paul Channon, who retained the seat until his own retirement in 1997. When the local Conservative Association selected him, the Countess (his grandmother) told them "I think you have done right by backing a colt when you know the stable he was trained in."

Gwendolen Guinness was not a feminist, believing, rather bizarrely given the nature of her family's long occupation of the Southend seat, that sex and class discrimination were becoming out of date. She died at her home in Surrey in 1966.

## Securing the Act

When the Representation of the People (Equal Representation) Bill was finally published, there was general – though not universal – agreement that the time had come for the issue of the franchise to be finally resolved. However, both in and outside parliament opposition remained, with women as well as men opposing an electoral roll in which men would be outnumbered, and much moral concern that the dress and behaviour of women under the age of twenty-five (i.e., 'flappers') might make them unfit for the exercise of a vote.

Inside parliament, men such as Sir William Joynson-Hicks, who as Home Secretary had spent large parts of the decade frustrating attempts to get a private member's bill passed, now found himself in the position of having to introduce the government's legislation and steer it through parliament as expeditiously as possible. And it was not an easy bill to steer, being viewed by the other parties as something of a curate's egg, and by a number of members on his own side, particularly in the House of Lords, as an anathema.

One of the problems was that both the Liberal and the Labour parties wanted other changes besides equalisation of the franchise. The Liberal Party, for instance, had a long commitment to electoral reform and proportional representation, and wanted to see it introduced as part of any change. For them, this had a higher priority than the women's vote and almost always had had, and they were unhappy not to find it included.

The Labour Party, on the other hand, wanted to end the practice of 'plural voting', by which business owners and some electors at universities had two votes. Far from achieving this, the bill actually proposed to extend plural voting to men and women on an equal basis, and some Labour members were uneasy at being asked to replace one manifest injustice with what they saw as another.

There had also been discussion throughout the decade about the age at which both men and women should be allowed to vote, and there was strong support in some quarters for equalising the franchise at twenty-five rather than twenty-one, thus granting the vote to women under thirty, but removing it from men under the age of twenty-five. It had been anticipated that the promised Speaker's Conference would examine this issue amongst others; the appearance of the bill in the absence of the Conference infuriated many Conservative MPs and peers.

Then there were concerns over the size of constituencies, which were growing larger, and the cost of election campaigns, which were increasing. The Home Secretary and the Prime Minister, Stanley Baldwin, would have to negotiate all these differing demands, and the proposed legislation would have to have enough in it for all parties to be able to support it.

In the event, the Bill which was published on 13 March 1928 was relatively successful in this. It equalised the voting age at twenty-one for both men and women, and abolished the property qualification for women as the 1918 Act had for men. Women were to get the business and university votes in their own right, as well as by virtue of their husbands having them, but 16,000 men whose wives owned businesses which qualified for the business vote would also get it. It dealt with the issue of election expenses levels but did not introduce a constituency boundary review, and there was no mention of proportional representation.

Thus many Tories who had reservations about the lowering of the age limit for women reluctantly accepted its inevitability and were somewhat mollified by the extension of the business vote and the absence of any reference to proportional representation. The Liberals were dismayed at the absence of proportional representation, but did not feel sufficiently dismayed to vote against the equalisation of voting rights for men and women. Labour was opposed to the extension of plural voting but strongly supportive of the extension of the women's franchise. Members across all parties had concerns about levels of election expenses, and the sizes of constituencies, but the changes were not so great as to jeopardise the rest of the Bill, and most MPs of all parties chose either to be very supportive, or to have their say on their particular issue and then be supportive.

The Bill arrived at its Second Reading Stage in the House of Commons on 29 March 1928. It was moved by Sir William Joynson-Hicks, who observed with apparently unconscious irony that the Bill fulfilled 'what has been now for many years the aim of most parties in the House, including the Conservative Party', and said that he had the 'privilege to move what I hope will probably be the final reform'.

He went on to give a detailed account of the progression of electoral legislation over two centuries, suggesting – erroneously – throughout that this had been achieved by all parties working together in harmony for the greater good. He outlined what was actually in the Bill, and explained how it would tidy up the complicated situation which had existed since 1918. He explained that 5,250,000 women would be added to the roll, including 10,000 who would acquire the university franchise, 150,000 who would get the business vote through their husbands, and 31,000 who would get the business vote in their own right. There would also be a small number of men who would get the business vote by virtue of their wives being entitled to it. He outlined the timescale for the compilation of the new electoral register and dealt with arrangements for the exercise of the plural vote and for ensuring that nobody voted twice illegally.

He also gave details of the categories into which the five million plus women to be enfranchised fell. 1.8 million of them – 33% – were unmarried women over the age of thirty. A further 1.7 million were married women between the ages of twenty-one and thirty. There were nearly 1.5 million 'occupied' (i.e., employed) unmarried women between those ages, 175,000 'unoccupied' single women aged between twenty-five and thirty and finally 216,000 'unoccupied' single women aged between twenty-one and twenty-five. This last group was the one which caused much of the controversy, being generally regarded as irresponsible and untrustworthy; the term 'flapper' (which now evokes a whole generation) was then regarded as a term of abuse – Joynson-Hicks referred to it as 'opprobrious'.

He concluded his speech by saying that some people seemed to be concerned that, if these women were added to the register, they would not vote Conservative, and that, in his opinion, this was a disgraceful reason for voting against the Bill. 'That is not a position I am prepared to discuss either inside or outside this House,' he said. 'It does not in the least matter which way they vote. We are doing what we believe to be right, and I ask the House to pass this Bill by an overwhelming majority.'

Philip Snowden, speaking for the Labour Party, said that he wholeheartedly supported the Bill, but could not resist pointing out that he could not find any record of either the Prime Minister (Stanley Baldwin) or the Home Secretary ever having supported women's suffrage in any form until very recently. However, he agreed that the Bill completed the extension of the franchise, although he also took the opportunity to object to the continuation of plural voting, remarking that 'If you are going to have manhood and womanhood as the basis of your franchise, you have no logical justification for maintaining in your electoral system, a qualification of a different character.'

He concluded by saying, 'We support (this Bill) not merely in the interests of the women themselves, but because we believe it will bring a truer comradeship and closer cooperation between men and women in the common task of grappling with the grave national questions which it is the duty of enfranchised democracy to solve.'

After this Brigadier-General Sir George Cockerill, the MP for Reigate, rose to move an amendment and to oppose the Bill. Having described himself as 'more of a feminist than the right hon Gentleman himself', he proceeded to put the case for male superiority, and for the unfairness of making women a majority of the electorate. He also said that most women opposed the reform (an argument familiar to all women who have campaigned for equality before and since), and observed that, although more boys were born each year than girls, boys were less likely to reach maturity. 'The trouble is,' he said 'that the higher the organism, the more difficult it is to rear it.'

He continued for some time in a similar vein, punctuated by Nancy Astor either heckling or responding to his rhetorical questions.

| Cockerill: | I ask, has man less spirit, less vision (than woman)? |
| --- | --- |
| Astor: | Yes |

The amendment was seconded rather more forcibly by Colonel Applin, who seems to have been almost incoherently outraged by the whole idea of voting.

> 'I do not look upon the vote as a gift. I do not look upon it as a right. It is not a right for any individual. The individual who is not capable or fit ought not to have a vote. I have been deprived of a vote all my life because I am a soldier. I have never complained. I have never run round saying "I am injured because I have no vote." What would my vote do for me? Absolutely nothing. It is not a right; it is a duty. I have never in my life voted for a Member of Parliament......'

He spoke at considerable length, giving a number of reasons for opposing the measure including the suggestion that Muslim subjects of the Empire would be upset to be governed by a majority of women, and observing – one cannot help feeling with some approval – that 'among the Mohammedans, women not only have no voice, but are not seen.' Finally, however, he provoked the ire of the Labour MP Ellen Wilkinson.

| Applin: | ... Hitherto, men have done all the heavy work in this country. |
| --- | --- |
| Wilkinson: | Oh really! Good gracious! |
| Applin: | You find no women in the stokehold of a ship or in the Navy; you find no women down the coal mines today .... it (the vote) must involve going into the rough and tumble of life. It must mean taking on grave responsibilities, which would perhaps be too great a burden for women. |
| Wilkinson: | indicated dissent |
| Applin: | ... Suppose a woman sat on that bench as Chancellor of the Exchequer? |
| Wilkinson: | Why not? |
| Applin: | Imagine her introducing her Budget, and in the middle of her speech a message coming in "Your child is dangerously ill, come at once." I should like to know how much of that Budget the House would get, and what the figures would be like....' |

The Countess of Iveagh, who spoke next, observed that she would like to see Colonel Applin 'make that statement (that women do not take part in the heavy work of the nation) before a large audience of married women and observe the effect.' Ellen Wilkinson, in her own speech, reminded him that 'as a matter of fact, in every Province of India today, women already have the vote.' She also returned to the argument about the Chancellor of the Exchequer.

'... But suppose that, say, the present Chancellor of the Exchequer received during his Budget speech a message to say that his child was ill, what would he feel like? Would he not have exactly the same feelings as the mother, and would he not do the duty that he had to do by his country and go on with his speech, as many other people have had to do?'

She also took up the issue of the language used to describe women – particularly young women:

'There is a curious reluctance, especially in the Press, to admit the maturity of women. ...There seems to be a determination that in some way it is ungallant to describe a woman as a woman and not a girl ...'

Later in the debate Nancy Astor also objected to the use of the word 'females' to describe women, observing that 'in the first chapter of Genesis man is neither male nor female, but is made in the image of God.'

Of the seven women MPs, four – Nancy Astor, Ellen Wilkinson, Margaret Bondfield and the Countess of Iveagh – spoke in what turned out to be a very long debate. Of the remaining three, neither Susan Lawrence (who supported the Bill) nor Mabel Philipson (who, though opposed to it ultimately voted in favour) spoke, and the Duchess of Atholl (also opposed) appears not to have been present.

Ellen Wilkinson, having disposed of Colonel Applin's views on Muslim women as well as the matter of the Chancellor of the Exchequer, turned to the question of women as mothers. She pointed out that women do not spend their whole lives bearing children, and that, as the tendency towards smaller families grew, time spent in this manner would grow less and less. She also remarked that there were over two million women who, for one reason or another, had to earn their own living and had no husband, but ought not to be excluded from the government of their country. Then she turned to the issue of the legislation before them, and its place in history.

'I speak with the feeling that, as one hon. Member has said, this is the closing of a great drama. I felt when I came into this House, and I think the other women Members must have felt too, that we had entered it as the result of the labours of some of the best women that this country or the world has known. Women have worked very hard. They have starved in prison, they have given their lives, or have given all their time, in order that women might sit in this House and take part in the legislation of the country. I need only mention honoured names like Josephine Butler, Lydia Becker, Emmeline Pethick-Lawrence, and Mrs. Fawcett to realise that that band of women, though they may never sit here, have made possible what we are doing to-day. I am glad this is not to be a party measure.

> 'I hope all Members will realise that we are doing at last a great act of justice to the women of the country. I do not think any one party is going to claim the allegiance of women, and I do not think it desirable that it should, but just as we have opened the door to the older women, to-night we are opening it to those who are just entering on the threshold of life and in whose hands is the new life of the future country that we are going to build. I feel it is a very solemn occasion, and I am glad that I have been allowed to take some part in it.'

Margaret Bondfield, who would later become Britain's first woman Cabinet minister, also welcomed the Bill, although she deplored the retention of plural voting. She commented on the view that only 'educated' people should be on the electoral roll, and challenged the traditional view of what education was.

> 'But what is his definition of "educated"? If he means by that persons who have had the opportunity to attend certain categories of schools, I absolutely and entirely disagree with him. I think in connection with the political work of our country we can take the experience of the workman's wife and daughter, educated in the university of experience, who have had to face the hardships, ugliness and suffering which surrounds so much of our social conditions to-day. They have the experience that very few people who have passed through universities have. We want, to bring into our political life and into the general pool of experience that kind of education.'

She also accurately predicted the form which women's participation in politics would take, and refuted the notion that because women would outnumber men on the electoral roll, women would necessarily effectively make all the decisions.

> 'It is not as if all women will take one point of view and all men will take another point of view. It is absolutely impossible to conceive of any subject in which that kind of division would occur. What will happen will be that the Conservative women and the Conservative men will or may take a different angle on a question which would be regarded by us as a purely Conservative party question. The same thing will apply with regard to Labour women and Labour men and Liberal women and Liberal men. It all adds to the strength of the State.'

The Countess of Iveagh was brief in her contribution, but very much to the point. She welcomed the Bill, dealt with one or two of the objections to it, and then came on to the matter of there being more women electors than men. In doing this, she put her finger onto one of the issues which has remained a problem ever since.

> 'If it were really likely that there would be anything approaching to a division of the sexes as sexes on any public question, we should

surely have seen some indication of it since the last extension of the franchise, which brought in women for the first time. I can only speak for the party which I represent, but I think the statement cannot be challenged that though women are politically better organised than men, are politically much more active than men, it is extremely difficult to get a woman candidate adopted in a constituency. I believe that to be the case with other parties as well as our own.'

Finally, and relatively late in the debate, Nancy Astor spoke. After a few swipes at the Press she paid tribute to the women who had fought for the vote, and then turned to the opponents of the Bill. Referring to the members who were supporting the amendment she said:

'We realise that [this] is the swan song of the die-hards. They may be singing like swans, but they are thinking like geese. It is as though they set back the hands of their watches, thinking by doing so that they were changing Greenwich time. The Amendment is based on fear. They are frightened of light; they are frightened of reason; and they are frightened of progress. Progress comes in spite of faint-hearted men. We know all reforms have been hampered by people who were afraid, but this woman question has had wonderfully stout-hearted women who first saw the vision and fought for it. They have been women of high moral and spiritual outlook. The coming of women into public life is not really, as our friends fear, revolution. It is simply evolution.'

In a speech which rambled through history ('It is interesting to know that some women under Egyptian laws had more property freedom than the women of England had until fifty years ago'), the relative merits of eastern religions and Christianity, and various Bible stories, she observed that 'a civilisation is judged by the status of women in a country' and that:

'It is in trying to divide mankind into sexes and keeping them in these divisions that so many of our troubles have come. An hon. Gentleman has asked whether there is not a woman's point of view. The truth is, that man is such a mixture of woman and man. Sometimes a woman may be moved by the male in her just as a man may be moved by the female in him. I think that people are beginning to see that, and the more they see it the more we shall progress. Men cannot go forward alone, and we know perfectly well that the men who are foremost in vision and outlook are the men who are influenced by good women.'

Finally, the Prime Minister, Stanley Baldwin, rose to support the Bill, and, at the end of a longish speech, concluded:

'The right hon. Member for Colne Valley (Mr. Snowden) was right. I used to vote against women's suffrage. I was taught by the War, which taught me many things. I learnt, I hope and believe, during that time when the young manhood of the nation was passing through the Valley of the Shadow of Death, to see such things as wealth, prosperity and worldly success in their proper proportion, and I realised as I never did before that to build up that broken work half the human race was not enough. It must be the men and women together. To-night marks the final stage in the union of men and women working together for the re-generation of their country and for the regeneration of the world. It may well be that by their common work together, each doing that for which they are the better fitted, they may provide such an environment that each immortal soul as it is born on this earth may have a fairer chance, and a fairer home than has ever been vouchsafed to the generations that have passed.'

After a debate which had lasted well over six hours, the House finally divided. 387 members, including all six of the women present, voted for the Bill, and ten members voted against. They included a Brigadier-General, three Colonels, a Lieutenant-Colonel, two Majors and a Captain. Four of these were also knights of the realm, as were two others.

In May, the Bill received its second reading in the House of Lords, where it was moved by the Lord Chancellor, Lord Hailsham, and where much the same pattern of debate ensued. In this case, however, there were no women's voices at all; women were not admitted to the House of Lords on any basis at all until 1958. 114 peers voted for the Bill, and 35 against.

After this, the Bill passed through its various remaining stages without much further delay, other than to revisit the issue of plural voting, and to look at various practical matters such as the compilation of the register, the size of constituencies, and the perennial matter of election expenses. It received the Royal Assent on 2 July 1928.

Within a year, the 5 million people it enfranchised got the opportunity to use their new right (or duty) as Stanley Baldwin's government fell, and the fourth general election in a decade – the first ever with universal suffrage – took place on 30 May 1929.

# Mabel Philipson

Mabel Philipson was born in 1886, and is an example of the different paths women took both into and out of political life in the twenties. She was also the first Conservative MP not to come of moneyed or titled stock, and the first woman MP with a disability.

She was brought up in modest circumstances, and after leaving school she started work in a theatre box office. Gradually she began to get small parts in plays, and in classic fashion, her break came when the actress she was understudying fell ill. Mabel stood in and was noticed, and thereafter quickly progressed into West End shows.

In 1911 she married a nephew of Cecil Rhodes, but was widowed by a car accident soon after. Although she lost the sight of an eye in the crash, she continued her stage career, and in 1917 married Hilton Philipson.

In 1922 he was elected to parliament for Berwick-upon-Tweed, but was removed when his agent was found to have broken electoral law on spending limits. Mabel stood in the by-election, but whereas Hilton had been a Liberal, she stood as a Conservative. She campaigned with flair, and won the seat, retaining it at the next general election with a greatly increased majority.

Regarded by other women as well as men as lightweight, Mabel worked doggedly for the issues which concerned her, and was responsible for legislation requiring nursing homes to be registered for the first time. But she opposed the extension of the franchise and was one of a number of MPs who met Mussolini in 1924. She also continued to appear on stage from time to time, usually for charity.

Mabel Philipson always considered herself as a stand-in rather than a politician in her own right, and when her husband's disbarment expired in 1929 she stood down, and Hilton Philipson returned to parliament in her place. She resumed her acting career, retiring from the stage in 1933. She died in 1951.

# Vera, Lady Terrington

Born Vera Bousher in 1889, she married young but divorced her first husband in 1912. In 1918, she married her second, Harold Woodhouse, Lord Terrington, and shortly after began her brief political career.

In 1922, she stood as the Liberal candidate for Wycombe, but was defeated by the Conservatives. Undaunted, she stood again in December 1923 on a platform which included strong support for women's rights, and won with a majority of 1,682, thus becoming the first in what was to become a long line of women MPs in highly marginal seats. She was also one of the first women MPs not to have 'inherited' their seats from their husbands.

During the course of the campaign she was profiled in the Daily Express under the headline 'Aim if Elected – Furs and Pearls', and although she had rather invited this by telling the journalist interviewing her that 'I shall put on my ospreys and my fur coat and my pearls... Every woman would do the same if she could. It is sheer hypocrisy to pretend in public life that you have no nice things...', she sued the paper on the grounds that the article had portrayed her as 'vain, frivolous, and an extravagant woman'. Unsurprisingly – if disappointingly – , she lost the case, the jury deciding that the dress of women MPs was indeed a matter of public interest.

In parliament, she supported the equalisation of guardianship rights for parents, the abolition of the means test for the pension, and legislation to prevent cruelty to animals.

In the 1924 general election, however, she lost her seat, and although she stood again in 1925 she did not return to parliament thereafter. She divorced Lord Terrington in 1926, and later emigrated to South Africa, where she married her third husband in 1949. She died in the mid nineteen-fifties.

# Part Two:

# The 'Flapper' Election

'...there is a fear that the young are likely to be less experienced and perhaps vote for one of the parties opposed to the present government. If youth lacks experience, it has two virtues to make up for it, courage and enthusiasm; and today these two virtues are every bit as essential to a political party as any other.'

Sir Hugh Lucas-Tooth (aged 25)
speaking in the debate on the second reading of the Bill, 29 March 1928.
At the time of his election in 1924, Sir Hugh, at 21, was one of the youngest MPs ever to be elected. During the debate he described himself as 'a species of male flapper'.

# The Election and the Women Who Won

The General Election of 30 May 1929 was fought in a darkening social, economic and political atmosphere. Following the War, unemployment had risen steadily, especially in the industrial areas of the country, and although the Wall Street crash was still four months away, the signs were ominous.

Stanley Baldwin's Conservatives fought the election under the slogan 'Safety First' and their election manifesto promised more of the policies they had been pursuing for the previous four and a half years. Labour accused the government of incompetence, inaction and reaction, but although they promised to deal with unemployment and the economic situation, they were vague as to how this would be done. Lloyd George and the Liberal Party – knowing that it was unlikely that they would be returned to government – were able to be more specific, promising (amongst other things) public works, free trade, and temperance reform.

At the previous election in 1924, thirty-nine women had stood for election; now, in 1929, this rose to sixty-nine – 4% of the total 1,730 candidates. The Conservative Party – which still felt, despite having guided the Act through parliament, that women were not suitable parliamentary candidates, and that parliament was not a suitable place for women – fielded only ten women candidates. The Liberal Party fielded twenty-five, and Labour thirty. The remaining four either stood for very minor parties, or as independents.

Although this represented a significant increase on earlier levels, it was still only a tiny proportion of candidates overall, and most of these women were standing in seats they had very little chance of winning. In the event, fourteen were successful – three Conservative (all sitting MPs seeking re-election), nine Labour, of whom six had never been elected before, one new Liberal, and one new Independent. Together, they constituted a mere 2% of MPs.

They were a very varied group. Some, such as the Duchess of Atholl, the Countess of Iveagh and Viscountess Astor, were society ladies. At the other end of the scale, Jennie Lee was a young woman of twenty-four from the Lanarkshire coal field. Between them they had experience of almost every facet of life – they included mothers and childless women, married women and spinsters, working women and women who had never needed to work, women with immense wealth and women with none at all. There were women with experience of social work, of local government and of ministerial office. Some of them were pioneers, whereas others found themselves in parliament almost by accident. Some would go on to have long and distinguished political careers, whilst others would lose their seats after only one term.

## The Flapper Election and After

This interesting and diverse group of women were:

| | | |
|---|---|---|
| Nancy, Viscountess Astor | Plymouth Sutton | Conservative |
| Ethel Bentham | Islington East | Labour |
| Margaret Bondfield | Wallsend | Labour |
| Gwendolen Guinness, Countess of Iveagh | Southend-on-Sea | Conservative |
| Mary Agnes Hamilton | Blackburn | Labour |
| Susan Lawrence | East Ham North | Labour |
| Jennie Lee | Lanarkshire North | Labour |
| Megan Lloyd-George | Anglesey | Liberal |
| Cynthia Mosley | Stoke-on-Trent | Labour |
| Marion Phillips | Sunderland | Labour |
| Edith Picton-Turbervill | The Wrekin | Labour |
| Eleanor Rathbone | Combined English Universities | Independent |
| Katharine Stewart-Murray, Duchess of Atholl | Perth & Kinross | Conservative |
| Ellen Wilkinson | Middlesbrough East | Labour |

Eight of them were new, the remaining six (Astor, Bondfield, Guinness, Lawrence, Stewart-Murray and Wilkinson) having been elected at various points during the 1920s.

The average age of the 1929 intake was forty-five, with Ethel Bentham the oldest at sixty-eight and Jennie Lee the youngest at twenty-four (although Megan Lloyd George, at twenty-seven, and Cynthia Mosley, at thirty, were also very young for parliamentarians). Five of the women were married (all three of the Conservatives, and two Labour members).

Sadly, there appears to be no known photograph of all fourteen women together. There seems to have been very little sense of the historic nature of the election, and perhaps, given the circumstances in which the election was held, this was not surprising. However, the 1929 election was notable for a number of reasons besides the record number of women.

# A Great Act of Justice

*Labour Women MPs in 1929 L-R Jennie Lee (back row) Marion Phillips, Edith Picton-Turbervill, Ethel Bentham, Mary Agnes Hamilton (front row) Susan Lawrence, Margaret Bondfield, Ellen Wilkinson, Cynthia Mosley*

For one thing, more people voted on 30 May 1929 than had ever voted before. In December 1910, at the last election before any women were enfranchised, there was an 82% turnout, but that represented fewer than five million votes. In the 1918 General Election, turnout (understandably, since many men were still at the Front), fell to 57%, but the number of people voting rose to more than ten million. In 1924, at the last election before universal suffrage, turnout was up to 77%, with nearly sixteen million electors participating, but in 1929, although turnout fell by 1%, over twenty-one and a half million votes were cast.

In other words, a substantial number of the women (and men) enfranchised by the 1928 Act used their vote. And to some extent they used it to justify the fears of some of the die-hard Conservatives who had suggested that young women might not be entirely disposed to vote for them.

Although the election resulted in a hung parliament, the Labour Party took a majority of the seats (287), closely followed by the Conservatives with 260. As a result, the Liberals held the balance of power with their fifty-nine MPs. Following the usual discussions, Labour's Ramsay Macdonald became Prime Minister again and appointed a cabinet which included Margaret Bondfield as Minister of Labour – the first woman to hold cabinet rank, and the first to be sworn in as a Privy Councillor.

However, although Labour had won most seats, they had not won the most votes, and this was one of the very few elections (the others being in 1951 and 1974) in which the government of the day took office having seen fewer people vote for them than for the main opposition party. In this case, Labour polled just over eight million votes, and the Conservatives nearly eight and a quarter million. Inevitably, this undermined the government's credibility from the start, and two years later in 1931 another election took place at which half of the women who succeeded in 1929 lost their seats.

# Margaret Bondfield

Margaret Bondfield led a crowded and pioneering life which began in 1873 in Somerset, where her father was a non-conformist lace-maker. Margaret began work at thirteen, initially as a pupil teacher, then as a shop assistant.

She soon became involved in the trade union movement, and began to research and write about the conditions of working women, particularly in the retail industry. Her rise through her union was meteoric – in 1898 at the age of twenty-five she was its assistant secretary and a year later she was the only woman delegate at the TUC, seconding the motion which set up the Labour Party.

She continued researching and campaigning on behalf of women workers, and in 1906 joined Mary Macarthur in setting up the National Federation of Women Workers. Amongst her many projects was research on the employment of married women and maternal and child welfare, and when state maternity benefits and improvements in medical care for women and their children were introduced in 1914, it was at least in part as a result of her work.

In 1918, Margaret was elected to the TUC General Council, and in 1923 became the first woman to chair it.

In 1920, 1922 and 1923 she stood for parliament in Northampton; at the third attempt she was successful and became one of the first Labour women MPs. She lost her seat a year later, but then won Wallsend in a by-election in 1926, remaining its MP until 1931. In 1924 she became the first woman minister, and in 1929 both the first woman cabinet minister and the first woman privy councillor. However, as Minister for Labour she was responsible for the Unemployment Insurance Fund and in 1931 supported the cutting of unemployment benefits; both of these measures were profoundly unpopular with both the Labour Party as a whole and the public, and contributed to the loss of her seat in 1931.

Margaret Bondfield was never a great friend of women's suffrage per se, but was passionately committed to equal and universal suffrage and to establishing the worth and dignity of women's roles and skills.

After losing her seat, she returned work for her trade union, retiring in 1938. She died in Surrey in 1953.

# Ethel Bentham

Ethel Bentham was one of the oldest women to be elected, getting into parliament at the age of sixty-eight. She was also the first woman to die whilst an MP, and the first woman MP to be succeeded by another woman at a by-election.

She was born in London of middle class parents, but grew up in Dublin, where she was educated to a high level. She studied medicine in London, Paris and Brussels, and practised as a doctor first in Newcastle and then in London.

There she became involved in the Labour Party, as well as in a campaign to establish a baby clinic in North Kensington. In 1912 she was elected to Kensington Borough Council, (upon which she sat until 1925) and in 1918 she became one of the first women magistrates.

In the same year the Women's Labour League, which she chaired, was absorbed by the Labour Party, and Ethel Bentham became a member of the National Executive. She became one of the first women to stand for parliament, standing unsuccessfully on three occasions during the 1920s.

In 1929, and at the age of sixty-eight, she was elected as the MP for Islington East.

In parliament she concentrated on health issues, but also spoke on judicial matters and issues relating to women's interests, and particularly on the nationality of married women.

Her time in parliament was cut short by her death in 1931 of influenza. In the subsequent by-election both the Labour and the Conservative Parties fielded women candidates. Labour won with Leah Manning (who was president of the National Union of Teachers), but the Conservatives' Thelma Cazalet took the seat in the general election later that year and held it until 1945.

High-profile within her party during her lifetime, Ethel Bentham was a woman who achieved a great deal in unpromising circumstances, but who is now largely forgotten. However, she remains a pioneer both in medicine and in politics, and her contribution to infant health in London alone was significant.

# Jennie Lee

Jennie Lee was one of the first working class women to be elected, and one of the youngest. She was born into a mining community in Fife in 1904 and grew up surrounded by trade union and Labour politics, but her drive and abilities won her scholarships to the University of Edinburgh, from which she eventually graduated with a law degree, an MA and a teaching certificate.

In February 1929 (before she could actually vote), she won North Lanark in a by-election, retaining it in the general election in May. She lost her seat in 1931, and was then out of parliament until 1945.

However, between those years she remained actively involved in the Labour movement, continuing to oppose Ramsay Macdonald's coalition, remaining a member of the Independent Labour Party (ILP) when it disaffiliated from the Labour Party in 1932, and standing against a Labour candidate in North Lanarkshire in 1935. She also met and in 1934 married Aneurin (Nye) Bevin.

When the Second World War broke out she campaigned for support for the Soviet Union and travelled to the United States to urge the American government to join the War. In 1942 she finally resigned from the ILP and in 1944 rejoined the Labour Party. In 1945 she won the seat in Cannock, and then remained an MP until 1970.

Like many women both then and now, Jennie Lee viewed feminism with suspicion, seeing it as a middle class cause and believing that the advancement of women was inextricably linked to the wider struggle for economic and social rights.

Nye Bevin's death in 1960 opened the way for her to be more active in her own right, and in 1964 she became Minister for the Arts in Harold Wilson's government, going on to hold a succession of ministerial posts. She was very much involved in the development of the Open University, which remains her great achievement.

Jennie became a privy councillor in 1966 and Chair of the Labour Party in 1967. When she lost her seat in 1970 she was created Baroness Lee of Asheridge and remained active both as a peer and as a writer. She died in 1988.

## A Great Act of Justice

# Megan Lloyd George

Megan Lloyd George, for many years the only Liberal woman MP, was the daughter of prime minister and Liberal leader David Lloyd George. She was born in 1902 and educated privately (her father's mistress was her governess) and at finishing school in Paris.

For some years she acted as her father's hostess, but was also politically active in her own right, and in 1929 was elected as the Liberal MP for Anglesey. From the outset she had much in common with elements of the Labour Party, and supported many of their policies. She also opposed Ramsay MacDonald's National Government.

At the same time, she supported her father and his attempts to revive the flagging Liberal Party, and continued to accompany him on foreign visits. As the nineteen thirties wore on she became increasingly opposed to appeasement, particularly after the Italian invasion of Abyssinia.

During the Second World War she served on various parliamentary committees, and in 1944 was a member of the Speaker's Conference on electoral reform, a measure which the Liberal Party had consistently supported. She campaigned for equal pay and for women's employment rights, as well as on other women's issues.

After the War she became deputy leader of the Liberal Party and worked to prevent what she saw as its rightwards shift. At the beginning of the nineteen fifties she began voting more and more with Labour, causing consternation in the Liberal ranks. She was defeated by Labour in the 1951 general election.

She remained committed to Wales and Welsh issues throughout her life, serving as president of the campaign for a Welsh parliament and becoming the first woman to be a Commissioner of the Church of Wales.

Her twenty-year long relationship with Phillip Noel-Baker, a prominent Labour MP, ended in 1956, and she never married.

In 1955 she defected to the Labour Party, winning Carmarthen in a 1957 by-election. She remained in the House as a Labour MP until her death in Wales in 1966.

# Marion Phillips

Marion Phillips, the Labour Party's first Women's Officer, was born in 1881 in Melbourne, Australia, where she was educated at home and, later, at college. In 1904 she went to study at the London School of Economics, from which she graduated with a doctorate in 1907.

She was employed in various capacities, both as a researcher (for a time by Beatrice Webb, with whom she subsequently disagreed on a number of issues), and then as a lecturer. In 1912 she became a councillor in Kensington, joining Ethel Bentham, with whom she shared a house.

Almost immediately, she became involved in Labour politics, both in women's organizations and the mainstream party. She worked hard, and demonstrated both commitment and organizational ability, but she also displayed an intellectual arrogance which made her unpopular with both women and men alike. However, she was passionately devoted to the Labour Party, and strongly believed that the class struggle came before all others. As a result, when the Labour Party absorbed its peripheral women's organizations in 1918, she was key to the process, becoming Labour's first National Women's Officer.

In this capacity she worked both to organize women workers and to get more women elected. She was very supportive of separate political organizations for women, and her energy and dedication ensured that hundreds of women's sections were set up across the country in a matter of months. However, she opposed cross-party working for women MPs during the 1920s, and on some issues – for instance, birth control – put the perceived interests of her party above those of women.

In 1929 Marion Phillips stood for one of the two seats in Sunderland, and was elected. Her seriousness, her dedication, and her fierce commitment to working men and women made her hugely popular with her electorate, and in parliament she was assiduous on their behalf. Although she was the first Australian woman to be elected, she showed no interest in colonial or empire policy except as it affected her constituents, and she spoke on free trade, working hours and industrial issues.

Despite her popularity, however, she lost her seat in 1931. She died of stomach cancer in London in 1932, aged only 51.

A Great Act of Justice

# Edith Picton-Turbervill

Edith Picton-Turbervill was born in Herefordshire in 1872, the daughter of an Indian army officer. She received a conventional education, but after a religious experience trained as a missionary and worked for the YWCA in India. After a serious illness she returned to London.

She continued to work for the YWCA, but also increasingly became involved in the non-militant wing of the suffrage movement, and, later, in war work, for which she was awarded an OBE. In 1919 she joined the Labour Party.

She contested parliamentary seats in both 1922 and 1924, but was unsuccessful on both occasions, In 1929 she was elected for the Wrekin, in Shropshire.

Her parliamentary interests reflected her religious and social convictions, and she was associated with developments both at home and in the colonies. Unlike some of the other Labour women, she was prepared to work across party lines where she thought it appropriate.

In 1931 she lost her seat, having refused to join the National Labour contingent. After this, she concentrated her efforts on improving the lot of women and children in the colonies, and worked particularly on the issue of child 'slavery' in the Far East. During the Second World War she returned to London and worked for the Ministry of Information.

Edith Picton-Turbervill was in many ways – and despite appearances – a woman of revolutionary views well ahead of her times. She campaigned for the ordination of women and openly and frequently criticised the church. She believed that women had something unique to offer, and applied this to politics as well as to religion.

She died in Gloucestershire in 1960.

# Mary Agnes Hamilton

Born in 1882 in Manchester, the daughter of a university professor and one of the first women to have studied at Newnham College, Cambridge, Mary Agnes Hamilton was educated in Scotland and at Cambridge. She worked first as an academic, and then, from 1913, as a journalist on the *Economist* magazine.

In 1905 she married Charles Hamilton but separated soon after.

In 1914 she joined the Independent Labour Party, and first stood for parliament in Rochester and Chatham in 1923. In 1924 she stood in Blackburn, and was defeated, but stood again in 1929 and was elected with the highest number of votes won by any woman candidate in that election.

Almost immediately, she was appointed a parliamentary private secretary, and secured the liking and respect of other MPs for both her ability and her personality. She was a delegate to the League of Nations and served on the Royal Commission on the Civil Service. She became increasingly uneasy, however, with the government's approach to unemployment, and she lost her seat in the 1931 election.

After this she concentrated on her other interests, in particular international questions. She was a frequent broadcaster, having presented the first edition of The Week in Westminster for the BBC in 1929. She saw the threat from Nazi Germany at an early stage, and although she had opposed the First World War, was an active advocate of sanctions and other action prior to the second.

During the War she became a civil servant, rising to head the United Nations Section. Afterwards, she continued to write, broadcast and lecture, particularly in the United States, and wrote biographies of Margaret Bondfield and Arthur Henderson, as well as autobiographical works.

Mary Agnes (or Molly, as she was usually known) Hamilton was an active and engaging figure; as an MP she always wore red shoes in the House, contrasting with the very sober 'uniform' then (and sometimes now) expected of women parliamentarians.

She died in London in 1966.

A Great Act of Justice

# The Women Who Lost

Sixty-eight women stood for parliament in 1929, and although only fourteen of them were actually elected, many of the rest had long histories in public life, education, trade unions, suffrage work or the professions, and all were pioneers in their way.

These are the women who lost, together with their constituencies and parties and their professions/interests as given in the Times House of Commons volume for that election.

|  | **Party** | **Constituency** | **Information** |
| --- | --- | --- | --- |
| Mrs C B Alderton | Liberal | Hull North West | Mayor of Colchester 1923-1924, President of the Congregational Women's Guild 1926-1928, national president of the Sisterhood Movement, borough and county councillor. |
| Lady Clare Annesley | Lab | Bristol West | Social worker. Former Secretary of Paddington Branch of Union of Democratic Control, member of the Executive of the Women's International League. |
| Eleanor Barton | Lab | Nottingham Central | Former Sheffield councillor, General Secretary of Women's Co-Operative Guild, expert on child welfare. |
| Mrs B A Bayfield | Lib | Manchester Gorton | Director of Manchester & Salford Cooperative Society |
| Margaret Beavan | Con | Liverpool Everton | Social worker in Liverpool. Councillor since 1921, Lord Mayor 1927-28. Formed Liverpool Child Welfare Association in 1901. |
| Mrs H Bell | Lab | Luton | Teacher and St Pancras councillor. |
| Barbara Bliss | Lib | East Grinstead | Educated at Girton College, Cambridge, worked as a nurse in the War and with refugees in Constantinople. |
| Mrs C E M Borrett | Lab | Weston-super-Mare | Formerly a London school teacher. |

*The Women Who Lost (cont'd)*

| | | | |
|---|---|---|---|
| Isabel Brown | Comm | Motherwell | Teacher, lived in Russia between 1921 and 1926, returning for the General Strike, during which she was imprisoned. |
| Dr Stella Churchill | Lab | Brentford & Chiswick | Educated at Girton College, Cambridge and London School of Medicine for Women. London County Councillor and author of several technical works. |
| Miss G M Colman | Lab | Hythe | Educated at Newnham College Cambridge, member of University Socialist Society. Tutor at Ruskin College, Oxford, and subsequently at the Workers' Educational Association in London. |
| Margaret Corbett Ashby | Lib | Hendon | Active suffragist, President of the International Women's Suffrage Alliance. Worked for welfare, education and equal citizenship. |
| Miss M G Cowan | Con | Paisley | Educated at Girton College Cambridge, Paris and Edinburgh Universities. Convenor and chair of Edinburgh Higher Education Committee and member of National Committee on the Training of Teachers. |
| Helen Crawfurd | Comm | Bothwell | Militant suffragette, Glasgow Secretary of the International Women's League, active in the rent strike of 1915, member of the Independent Labour Party, but joined the Communist Party in 1921. |
| Lady Crosfield | Lib | Islington North | Chair of North Islington Infant Welfare Centre. |

*The Women Who Lost (cont'd)*

| | | | |
|---|---|---|---|
| Mrs J Davies | Lab | Wells | Trade unionist and Labour activist. Member of the Bristol Board of Guardians |
| Mrs R Davies | Lab | Honiton | Alderman and JP in Aberdare. Formerly a schoolmistress, wife of a schoolmaster. |
| Elizabeth Edwardes | Lib | St Pancras South East | Former Vice Chair of London Young Liberal Federation. |
| Miss A Garland | Lib | Warrington | Member of Executive of Women's National Liberal Association, fought Portsmouth South in 1918. |
| Helen Gault | Lab | Perth | Teacher closely associated with the Cooperative movement in the West of Scotland. |
| Morgan Gibbon | Lib | Hackney South | Novelist, educated at Girton College, Cambridge. |
| Barbara Ayrton Gould | Lab | Northwich | Active in women's organizations for many years. Stood unsuccessfully in 1924. |
| Miss M P Grant | Lib | Salford West | Formerly a missionary, a nurse and a policewoman. Contested Leeds South East in 1922 and Pontefract in 1923. |
| Mrs Hoffman | Lib | Norfolk North | American, became a British citizen in 1928, interested in horticulture and agriculture. |
| Hester Holland | Lib | Hythe | Worker at Liberal Head Office and studied social conditions. |
| Beta Hornabrook | Lib | Birmingham Deritend | Ex-president of Wesleyan Conference, financial organizer for YWCA, Plymouth City councillor and member of Devonport Board of Guardians. |
| Dorothy Jewson | Lab | Norwich | Elected 1923, defeated 1924. |

## The Women Who Lost (cont'd)

| | | | |
|---|---|---|---|
| Miss M L K Jones | Con | Manchester Ardwick | Manchester City Councillor and governor of Manchester High School. Fought seat in 1924. |
| Frances Louise Josephy | Lib | Winchester | Aged 29. Cambridge honours degree in Classics. Research Secretary to the Radical Parliamentary Group in House of Commons. |
| Miss H M Keynes | Lab | Horsham & Worthing | Member of the Fabian Society. Contested Epsom in a by-election. |
| Enid Lapthorn | Lib | Hitchin | Former secretary to British Passport Office in Prague, and translator in Guaranty Trust Company, New York. Secretary of Liberal Social Council 1924-1926. |
| Miss M E Marshall | Lib | Smethwick | Social worker and former civil servant organizing women and juveniles for the Ministry of Labour. |
| Mrs Speedwell Massingham | Lab | Petersfield | Educated at London and University of Reading. Formerly on the stage. |
| Mrs Masterman | Lib | Salisbury | Author and literary editor of 'Outlook'. |
| Betty Morgan | Lib | Sunderland | BA at University of Wales, PhD from the Sorbonne. Active Liberal worker in South Wales. |
| Hon Mary A Pickford | Con | Farnworth | Formerly a Factory Inspector, and member of various Imperial Committees. |
| Anne Grace Roberts | Lib | Caerphilly | Expert on conditions in the South Wales mining area. Welsh nationalist and expert on Welsh language and literature. |
| Hilda Runciman | Lib | Tavistock | Formerly MP for St. Ives, which her husband won at this election. |

# A Great Act of Justice

### *The Women Who Lost (cont'd)*

| | | | |
|---|---|---|---|
| Alexandra Helen Schilzzi | Lib | Northampton | Aged 25. Lecturer for the League of Nations Union. |
| Helen B Shaw | Con | Bothwell | Previously stood in 1924, widow of officer killed in the War. |
| Clarice McNab Shaw | Lab | Ayr | First woman member of Leith Town Council, and a member of a number of public boards, including the Ayrshire Education Authority. Member of the Scottish Labour Executive. |
| Rosina Smith | Comm | Mansfield | Former schoolteacher, Communist leader, factory worker organizing women workers. |
| Kate Spurrell | Lab | Totnes | Plymouth schoolteacher. On Executive of NUT, and president in 1922. |
| Miss J Stephen | Lab | Portsmouth South | Secretary of the Home and Hotel Workers' Union, member of Bermondsey Council and the Bermondsey Guardians. |
| Lady Frances Henrietta Stewart | Lib | Kensington North | Hon Secretary of the National Indian Association, interested in infant and school welfare work. |
| Miss E Stewart | Lab | Edinburgh North | Factory worker at 14 and subsequently overseer. Women's Organizer in the Workers' Union for Scotland. |
| Ida Swinburne | Lib | Surrey East | Interested in industrial questions, free trade and education. Former council candidate. |
| Mrs R Townsend | Lab | Wycombe | Journalist, former Chair of Hammersmith Labour Party's Women's Section. |

*The Women Who Lost (cont'd)*

| | | | |
|---|---|---|---|
| Mrs C M Wadham | Lab | Lewisham West | Member of Lewisham Borough Council and Lewisham Board of Guardians. |
| Irene Ward | Con | Morpeth | CBE, stood unsuccessfully in 1924, interested in industrial matters. |
| Dora West | Lib | Bermondsey Rotherhithe | OBE, first Secretary of the League of Nations Union, formerly private Secretary to Liberal government minister. |
| Monica Whatley | Lab | St Albans | Eldest daughter of Major Pepys Whatley, great great grand-niece of an Archbishop. |
| Florence Widdowson | Lab | Rushcliffe | Methodist lay preacher at 16, and led various missions. Later became a teacher and joined Labour after the War. |
| May Gordon Williams | Con | Pontypridd | Became a barrister at the age of 22, in chambers in Liverpool. |
| Margaret Wintringham | Lib | Louth | Former MP for Louth – see separate biographical note. |

# Part Three:

# What Happened Next

*'I can only speak for the party which I represent, but I think the statement cannot be challenged that though women are politically better organised than men, are politically much more active than men, it is extremely difficult to get a woman candidate adopted in a constituency. I believe that to be the case with other parties as well as our own.'*

Gwendolen Guinness, Countess of Iveagh MP
speaking in the debate on the second reading of the Bill,
29 March 1928.

# The Thirties

After 1929, the specific issue of women's place in politics receded – at least for a time – and women became increasingly drawn into party political as opposed to cross-party activity. Only one woman MP – Eleanor Rathbone – remained resolutely independent, and although others such as Nancy Astor and the Duchess of Atholl had reputations as political mavericks, their very unreliability restricted their careers, as the chief requirement of any female MP was that she should be unyieldingly loyal and as indistinguishable from her male colleagues as possible. The political party system both encouraged and enforced this trend.

Initially, however, the problem for the parties was what to do with the women who had begun to join their ranks. There had always been women's party political organizations, but women had not been members of political parties themselves (even where such membership structures existed for men), and the problem of what to do with them after the franchise had been won was one which exercised all the parties to some degree.

The Women's Liberal Federation (WLF) had been set up in 1887, mainly to campaign for the franchise. After the First World War, its membership was relatively high, but this could not be sustained in the face of much more aggressive recruitment tactics by both the Labour and the Conservative parties, which, combined with the Liberal Party's increasingly poor electoral performance during the nineteen-twenties, saw WLF membership fall. Because there was a paucity of Liberal safe seats (and because those that there were always chose male candidates), Megan Lloyd George was, between 1929 and 1951, the only Liberal woman MP.

This absence of women meant that the Liberal Party was both least affected by the influx of women into politics and least exercised by the challenges that this brought. The other two parties, however, were much more concerned by the new political climate.

The Conservative Party had had women's structures and organizations either associated with it or contained within it for almost a century, but despite this was not encouraging to women candidates, and right from the start it was harder for women to get selected as Conservative candidates.

Meanwhile the Women's Labour League, set up in 1906 to be supportive, though not part, of the emerging Labour Party was dissolved in 1918, with women being admitted to membership of the Party in a subordinate role and without an independent organization.

And it was the Labour Party which, during the nineteen-twenties and thirties, increasingly argued that women should put party first and the wider women's movement second. There was a strong view that the needs of the working class as a whole had to be put before those of women, partly because of a belief that if class issues were resolved, those relating to gender would automatically follow, and partly because feminism was seen as a product of middle class women's struggles, which bore no relation to those of their poorer sisters. This did not mean that all Labour women were opposed to the women's movement, and the party's National Women's Organizer, Marion Phillips (elected to parliament in 1929 and defeated in 1931) was particularly keen to see women take their place in the mainstream of politics. But Labour was nevertheless in the forefront of increasing the polarization of women along party lines. The differing ways in which the parties fared in the two general elections in this decade (1931 and 1935) had a direct effect on how many, and which, women found themselves elected.

A total of twenty-one women were sent to parliament in the thirties. Five had first been elected prior to 1931. At the 1931 election, a total of fifteen were elected, but in 1935 this reduced to nine. Six of the twenty-one women were elected at by-elections in 1930 (Norfolk North), 1931 (Islington East), 1937 (Hemel Hempstead and Glasgow Springburn) and 1938 (Dartford and Fulham West).

Although the difference between nine and fifteen is large in itself, it is negligible in terms of the overall composition of the House of Commons. There were, however, significant changes in terms of the parties to which women MPs belonged. All nine of Labour's women lost their seats in 1931, with the result that between then and 1935 there were no Labour women at all in the House. On the other hand, thirteen Conservative women were elected, of whom seven lost their seats in 1935. One Liberal – Megan Lloyd George – was elected in both 1931 and 1935, and indeed continued to be the only Liberal woman until 1951, when she lost her seat – there were then none at all until the election of Ray Michie in Argyll & Bute in 1987.

Some women MPs developed a fame – or notoriety – far beyond that of simply being a woman in a man's world. Ellen Wilkinson, for instance, is still largely remembered for her association with the Jarrow Hunger March, and Eleanor Rathbone for her work on social and family issues. Nancy Astor continued to attract attention for both her eccentricities and her society life, and the Duchess of Atholl for her forceful – if unlikely – opposition to Franco in Spain. But overall women remained at the margins of politics, and after Margaret Bondfield lost her seat in 1931, there were no further women cabinet ministers until Ellen Wilkinson became Minister of Education in 1945.

The thirties established a pattern which endured at least until 1997, and which still to some extent exists today. Women on the whole were more likely to be fielded by their parties in marginal seats, and therefore more likely to benefit from or fall victim to their parties' varying fortunes. They could – and did – achieve ministerial status, but were unlikely to enter the Cabinet. They had a presence in the nation's political life, but it was not large, and many were known for what they did outside parliament rather than their contributions in it. They were under considerable pressure – from their parties as well as other sources – to conform to the male political stereotypes and systems already existing, and this pressure extended to dress and manner as well as to loyalty and ideology. Yet despite this, they managed to get legislation passed which slowly changed women's lives, and all of them — even those who were not feminists or were actively opposed to feminism — contributed to advancing women's interests.

Meanwhile, as war loomed, women continued to make advances in various professions. Lilian Wyles became the first woman Chief Inspector of Police in 1932, and in 1935 Dame Lilian Barker was appointed Assistant Commissioner of Prisons with responsibility for women prisoners. A year later Dame Laura Knight became the first woman to be elected a full member of the Royal Academy of Arts, (although a ban on women at their Annual Dinner meant that she was not actually invited to it until 1967).

Some careers remained closed to some women. Amongst others, the civil service, teaching and the BBC all continued to ban the employment of married women, and although women did gradually become more visible in some professions, they were never plentiful in any except those particularly 'suited' to them, such as nursing and, for single women, teaching.

The approach of war, however, prompted some women to think what their role in it might be going to be, and in 1938 the Women's Royal Voluntary Service and the Auxiliary Territorial Service were set up, followed in 1939 by the Women's Land Army. The scene for the next decade was set.

# Women Elected to Parliament in the 1930s

Two General Elections in the 1930s saw the number of women elected rise to fifteen in 1931, and fall back to nine in 1935. The list below shows all the women elected in this decade, and includes those elected at by-elections. The five women marked with an asterisk were first elected in previous parliaments (see earlier lists).

| | Party | Constituency | Elected in |
|---|---|---|---|
| Jennie Adamson | Lab | Dartford | 1938 (by-election) |
| Nancy, Viscountess Astor* | Con | Plymouth Sutton | 1931, 1935 |
| Lucy, Lady Noel-Buxton | Lab | Norfolk North | 1930** |
| Thelma Cazalet | Con | Islington East | 1931, 1935 |
| Ida Copeland | Con | Stoke-on-Trent | 1931 |
| Frances, Viscountess Davidson | Con | Hemel Hempstead | 1937 (by-election) |
| Marjorie Graves | Con | Hackney South | 1931 |
| Gwendolen Guinness, Countess of Iveagh* | Con | Southend-on-Sea | 1931 |
| Agnes Hardie | Lab | Glasgow Springburn | 1937 (by-election) |
| Florence Horsbrugh | Con | Dundee | 1931, 1935 |
| Megan Lloyd-George* | Lib | Anglesey | 1931, 1935 |
| Leah Manning | Lab | Islington East | 1931** |
| Mary Pickford | Con | Hammersmith North | 1931 |
| Eleanor Rathbone* | Ind | Combined English Universities | 1931, 1935 |
| Norah Runge | Con | Rotherhithe | 1931 |
| Helen Shaw | Con | Bothwell | 1931 |
| Katharine Stewart-Murray, (Duchess of Atholl)* | Con | Kinross & West Perthshire | 1931, 1935 |
| Edith Summerskill | Lab | Fulham West | 1938 (by-election) |
| Mavis Tate | Con | Willesden West, Frome | 1931, 1935 |
| Irene Ward | Con | Wallsend | 1931, 1935 |
| Sarah Ward | Con | Cannock | 1931 |
| Ellen Wilkinson | Lab | Jarrow | 1935 |

** elected at by-election and lost seat in subsequent general election

# Eleanor Rathbone

Eleanor Rathbone was born into a Liverpool political family in 1872. Her father, William Rathbone MP, together with Florence Nightingale, was responsible for establishing the district nursing system.

Eleanor grew up with a strong sense of public service, which continued when she went, amidst some parental unease, to Somerville Hall, Oxford to take a degree.

On returning to Liverpool she continued to work on the causes that motivated her – mainly the elimination of poverty and women's suffrage. In 1903 she began to work for the Victoria Women's Settlement, which was developing social services for women and children. Through this she met Elizabeth Macadam, who remained her lifelong friend and companion.

Throughout the early part of the twentieth century Eleanor worked on both practical measures to alleviate poverty and academic studies. She published a number of important papers and books, and was at the forefront of campaigning for measures such as widows' pensions and early forms of family allowances.

In 1909 she was elected to Liverpool Council, and remained a member until 1934, using the position to raise the profile of both suffrage and social issues in the city.

During and after the First World War, she and her colleagues piloted a variety of social measures, including the new state pension system, and after the War she became Secretary of the new Joint Universities Council on Social Studies. She was also elected president of the National Union of Societies for Equal Citizenship, which continued to campaign for the enfranchisement of all women.

In 1922 Eleanor stood unsuccessfully as an Independent candidate for East Toxteth, and in 1929 she was elected as the Independent MP for the Combined English Universities, a seat she held until 1946. As an MP she worked (not always very successfully) on women's issues in the Empire, and continued to campaign on social issues – she is particularly remembered for her work on family allowances. She also became involved in anti-fascism campaigns, and became an expert on refugees. During the Second World War she worked tirelessly both to help refugees and to protect interned German nationals in Britain.

She died suddenly in January 1946.

# Ellen Wilkinson

Ellen Wilkinson was born into a Methodist Manchester family in 1891, and was educated at local schools and at Manchester University, from which she graduated in 1913.

She was by then a member of the Independent Labour Party, and after she graduated she was appointed as an organiser for the National Union of Women's Suffrage Societies in Manchester. In 1915 she became the first woman national organiser for the shopworkers' union.

Opposed to the First World War, in 1920 she joined the newly founded Communist Party. In 1923 she became a Manchester City Councillor, and in the same year – the dividing lines between parties on the left being very fluid – stood unsuccessfully for Labour in Ashton-under-Lyne.

A year later she left the Communist Party and joined Labour. She was elected as the MP for Middlesbrough East in 1924, even though she herself could not actually vote. She retained the seat in 1929, but lost in 1931.

Like many other Labour women, Ellen Wilkinson believed that women's issues were inextricably bound up with the wider struggle for socialism. Her commitment to the politics of class led her to resist working with other women MPs across party lines, although she remained generally supportive of measures such as equal pay.

In 1935, she became the MP for Jarrow, and achieved lasting fame through her work with the Jarrow Hunger March. The experience more than confirmed her belief that capitalism could not solve the economic problems of the times, and the picture of 'Our Ellen', diminutive but determined, became part of the folklore of the North East.

Throughout the thirties, Ellen Wilkinson opposed fascism and appeasement, and during the War she served as a Parliamentary Secretary at the Ministry of Home Security (in which capacity she voted with the government against equal pay in 1944). In 1945 she became the first woman Minister of Education, and only the second woman to hold cabinet office. She implemented the 1944 Education Act and brought in, amongst other things, free school milk, a school leaving age of 15 and an expansion of further education.

She died in office in 1947, following heart failure.

# Cynthia Mosley

Cynthia Mosley is rarely thought of as an MP in her own right, yet she was one of the nine Labour women elected in 1929, achieved the highest swing to Labour in any seat in that election, and had one of the largest majorities of any women elected before 1945.

She was born into the aristocratic Curzon family in 1898, and for the first few years of her life lived in India, where her father was the Viceroy. Later she attended the London School of Economics, where she studied social work, and subsequently she worked in the East End of London.

In 1920 she married Oswald Mosley, then the Conservative MP for Harrow, whom she met during Nancy Astor's election campaign in 1919. In 1924, the couple joined the Labour Party, and Oswald subsequently won the seat at Smethwick in a by-election. In 1929, Cynthia stood as the Labour candidate in Stoke-on-Trent whilst her husband defended the Smethwick seat. Both were elected, and Oswald became a member of the government as the Chancellor of the Duchy of Lancaster.

In parliament, Cynthia followed up her early interest in social work and poverty, arguing in favour of widows' benefits and unemployment insurance and speaking up for unemployed women, who were often overlooked. She was popular with both her constituents and the wider public, and there was great dismay when, in 1930, she left the Labour Party to join Oswald Mosley's New Party. In 1931, when she stood down from parliament, Oswald stood in Stoke-on-Trent, and was heavily defeated.

In 1932 the New Party became the British Union of Fascists, and although Cynthia dutifully followed her husband in that also, her political life was effectively over. She died in London of peritonitis in 1933.

# The 1945 Election

The advent of the Second World War put an end to general elections for the time being, although by-elections were still held where vacancies occurred, and two women (Beatrice Wright in Bodmin in 1941 and Violet Bathurst, Lady Apsley in Bristol Central in 1943), were elected during the war period.

No women served in the wartime cabinet, although two served as ministers below that level. The Conservative Florence Horsbrugh was Parliamentary Secretary at the Ministry of Health throughout the War, whilst Labour's Ellen Wilkinson held the rank of Parliamentary Secretary first at the Ministry of Pensions and then, for the bulk of the War, at the Ministry of Home Security.

Political activity itself did not cease during this period, however, and the influx of women into the workforce meant that agitation for change in women's working and social conditions continued. In particular, equal pay continued to be an issue, and in 1940 the TUC finally pledged itself to work for it. In 1944 a Royal Commission (consisting of five men and four women) was set up to make recommendations. The ensuing report suggested that equal pay might be introduced for teachers and some civil service ranks, and there was a minority report produced by three of the women members who thought that it could also be extended into some parts of industry. By the time the report was published, in 1946, there was a new Labour Government seeking to avoid inflation in the aftermath of the war, and all of the proposals were therefore rejected.

In 1940, the pension age for women was reduced from 65 to 60, and one of the provisions of the 1944 Education Act lifted the ban on married women teachers. In 1946 the marriage bar was also abolished in the Civil Service and the Post Office. In 1945, Eleanor Rathbone at last saw the success of her long campaign for family allowances, which were the forerunner of the later child benefit.

In 1948, Cambridge opened its degrees fully to women; some colleges at both Oxford and Cambridge remained entirely male for decades to come. Dame Anne Loughlin became the first woman president of the TUC in 1943, Dame Lilian Penson became the first woman University Vice Chancellor at the University of London, and in 1949 Rose Heilbron became the first women King's Counsel.

The 1945 General Election – notable for so many reasons – saw a record number of women candidates – eighty-seven as opposed to the previous high of sixty-eight in 1929. The Conservative Party fielded fourteen women, Labour forty-one, and the Liberals twenty, leaving twelve women (including Eleanor Rathbone) standing as Independents or for small parties.

Twenty-four of these women were elected, more than in any other parliament, raising the percentage of women MPs from 1% in 1935 to 4%. There were twenty-one Labour women MPs, one Conservative woman, one Liberal and one Independent. Several of the new women elected – Barbara Castle, Bessie Braddock and Alice Bacon – would go on to become high-profile politicians. Some – Ellen Wilkinson and Eleanor Rathbone – were already household names. Jennie Lee had first won in 1929, then lost in 1931, and returned in 1945 to start a long and distinguished parliamentary career.

In the new Labour government, Ellen Wilkinson became only the second woman Cabinet Minister (as Minister of Education), and Jennie Adamson and Edith Summerskill became Parliamentary Secretaries. Women's presence at the highest levels was still low, but after 1945 persistent, and there were never again governments with no women in them at all.

# Women Elected to Parliament in the 1940s

The 1945 General Election saw a rise in the number of women MPs to 24 – the first time it had risen above 20. Women in this list who had been members of previous parliaments are indicated by an asterisk, and it includes women who won seats at by-elections.

|  | Party | Constituency | Elected in |
|---|---|---|---|
| Jennie Adamson | Lab | Dartford | 1938 (by-election) |
| Alice Bacon | Lab | Leeds | 1945 |
| Violet Bathurst, Lady Apsley | Con | Bristol Central | 1943 (by-election) |
| Bessie Braddock | Lab | Liverpool Exchange | 1945 |
| Lucy, Lady Noel-Buxton* | Lab | Norwich | 1945 |
| Barbara Castle | Lab | Blackburn | 1945 |
| Grace Colman | Lab | Tyneside | 1945 |
| Freda Corbet | Lab | Camberwell North West | 1945 |
| Alice Cullen | Lab | Glasgow Gorbals | 1948 (by-election) |
| Frances, Viscountess Davidson* | Con | Hemel Hempstead | 1945 |
| Caroline Ganley | Lab | Battersea South | 1945 |
| Barbara Gould | Lab | Hendon North | 1945 |
| Margaret Herbison | Lab | Lanarkshire North | 1945 |
| Jennie Lee* | Lab | Cannock | 1945 |
| Megan Lloyd-George* | Lib | Anglesey | 1945 |
| Jean Mann | Lab | Coatbridge | 1945 |
| Leah Manning* | Lab | Epping | 1945 |
| Lucy Middleton | Lab | Plymouth Sutton | 1945 |
| Muriel Nichol | Lab | Bradford North | 1945 |
| Florence Paton | Lab | Rushcliffe | 1945 |
| Eleanor Rathbone* | Ind | Combined English Universities | 1945 |
| Mabel Ridealgh | Lab | Ilford North | 1945 |
| Clarice Shaw | Lab | Ayrshire & Bute | 1945 |

*Women Elected in the 1940s (cont'd)*

| | | | |
|---|---|---|---|
| Edith Summerskill* | Lab | Fulham West | 1945 |
| Lady Tweedsmuir | Con | Aberdeen South | 1946 (by-election) |
| Ellen Wilkinson* | Lab | Jarrow | 1945 |
| Edith Wills | Lab | Birmingham Duddeston | 1945 |
| Beatrice Wright | Con | Bodmin | 1941 (by-election) |

# Bessie Braddock

Born in Liverpool in 1899 to a bookbinder and a campaigner against poverty, Bessie Bamber left school at fourteen and took jobs first in factories and then in shops.

Having been taken to her first political meeting before she was a month old Bessie gravitated naturally to political and trade union circles. There she met and married Jack Braddock, a Labour activist who later became Leader of Liverpool Council.

Like many others of her generation, Bessie joined the Independent Labour Party, then moved to the infant Communist Party, before settling into the Labour Party.

In 1930 she was elected to Liverpool Council and gained a reputation as a ferocious campaigner for the poorest people of the city. In 1936 she was selected to fight the Liverpool Exchange parliamentary seat, but the advent of the Second World War postponed the election until 1945.

She remained a fierce, uncompromising campaigner for the under-privileged, but she also campaigned on other issues, particularly mental health. However, some of her campaign techniques could be unorthodox; in 1952, in a bid to persuade the Home Secretary to ban air rifles, she fired one in the Chamber. Not surprisingly, she was the first woman MP to be suspended from the House.

Despite offers of ministerial office, Bessie Braddock chose to remain a back-bencher, believing that she could best serve 'her' people out of government. She did, however, serve on the National Executive of the Labour Party, and in 1947 was the Party's Vice Chair.

Although not renowned for her feminism, she understood only too well how women were judged by their looks, and her campaign to improve matters for larger women included appearing in a fashion show in 1959.

Her later years were mired in political infighting, and the Braddocks came to be regarded as synonymous with the right wing of the Labour Party, and, in Liverpool, as part of a 'corrupt' political machine.

Bessie Braddock died in November 1970, less than six months after ceasing to be an MP.

# A Great Act of Justice

# Barbara Castle

Barbara Betts was born in Chesterfield in 1910 and brought up in Yorkshire, where her father was a tax inspector. Both her parents were active members of the Independent Labour Party.

Educated at grammar school and Oxford, Barbara worked as a journalist during the War, marrying Ted Castle in 1944. In 1945, following years of political activity which included being one of the founders of *Tribune* magazine in 1937, she was elected as the MP for Blackburn.

Her ministerial career began almost immediately in the Ministry of Transport as an aide to Stafford Cripps, but she remained heavily identified with the left of the Party during the internal warfare of the nineteen fifties.

After Labour's victory in 1964 she became the first Minister for Overseas Development, moving to Transport in 1965 where she introduced compulsory seat belts, the breathalyser, and the 70 mph speed limit.

Her most controversial time, however, was at the Department of Employment, where she was responsible for both the Equal Pay Act (1970) and the white paper *In Place of Strife*. This attempted to reform industrial relations, caused a serious rift between the government and the trade unions, and for a time damaged Barbara's reputation as a left winger.

In 1974, following Labour's general election victory, she returned to government as Secretary of State for Social Services, where she established the link between earnings and pensions and introduced child benefits. She also, however, became embroiled in a dispute with health service staff which, for a time, closed accident and emergency departments.

In 1976 the new Prime Minister (James Callaghan aged 63), sacked Barbara Castle (aged 61) allegedly on the grounds that she was too old to be a Cabinet Minister. In 1979, Barbara became an MEP an office she held for 10 years before becoming Baroness Castle of Blackburn after her retirement in 1989.

To the end of her life in 2002 she remained a fierce campaigner for the causes she believed in, including the re-introduction of the link between pensions and earnings.

# Alice Bacon

Born in 1909, Alice Bacon was the daughter of a mining family in Normanton in Yorkshire, and was educated locally and at teacher training college in Kent. Throughout her life she kept her strong commitment to Yorkshire, retaining her accent long after others had lost theirs.

She was brought up in an intensely political atmosphere, and joined the Labour Party in her mid-teens. She also joined the Labour League of Youth and was soon an executive member of the Socialist Youth International. When she became a teacher she also became an active member of the National Union of Teachers. In 1941 she was the youngest woman ever to have been elected to the Labour Party's National Executive Committee, and she remained a member until her retirement in 1970.

In 1938 she was selected to fight the Leeds North East constituency, but, like many others, had to wait until 1945 to win the seat. She immediately became involved in the Committee inquiring into working hours and conditions in shops, mines and factories, and was a great advocate of the welfare state, the demolition of back-to-back housing, comprehensive education and the abolition of corporal punishment in schools. She also campaigned against capital punishment, introducing an unsuccessful bill to that effect in 1957.

In 1955 boundary changes led to her becoming the MP for Leeds South East. During the ninteteen fifties she was embroiled in the internecine warfare inside the Party – this was particularly strong in Leeds, where Hugh Gaitskell, the party leader, was also an MP. Alice Bacon remained loyal to the Party leadership throughout.

Despite this, when Labour returned to office in 1964 under the more left-wing Harold Wilson, Alice became Minister of State at the Home Office, and then in 1967 Minister of State for Education and Science, a job she thoroughly enjoyed.

In 1970 she became Baroness Bacon of Leeds and Normanton, and continued to be politically active. Most of her later years were spent in Yorkshire, and she died in 1993.

# The Fifties

Despite major events such as the Suez crisis, the nineteen fifties were a period of relative stability in terms of government – having the Conservatives in power for almost the whole decade – and saw a number of advances. Teachers achieved equal pay in 1953, and the first Permanent Secretary in the Civil Service was appointed in 1955 (Dame Evelyn Sharp). In 1958 the Life Peerages Act allowed the appointment of women peers, and Baroness Swanborough, Baroness Wootton and Lady Reading became the first to take their seats.

However, it was not a particularly fruitful period for the introduction of new women MPs – the general elections held in 1950, 1951, 1955 and 1959 contributed a total of only nineteen new women politicians to parliament, by far the best known of whom was Margaret Thatcher.

The general election of 1950, called after a full five years of Labour government, returned it with a majority reduced from 146 to 5, and it was therefore no surprise when little over a year later the country was at the polls again. This time the Conservatives won with a majority of seventeen and although this was narrow, it was enough to see them through until 1955, when Anthony Eden's government was returned with a much increased majority of fifty-four.

In 1957 Harold Macmillan became Prime Minister, and two years later the 1959 general election produced a record twenty-six women MPs. Of these women, thirteen were Labour, eleven Conservative, and the remaining two were Ulster Unionists.

One of the interesting features of the decade was the presence of the two Northern Irish women MPs. Patricia Ford had 'inherited' her North Down seat from her father, whilst Patricia McLaughlin had been educated at Dublin's Trinity College and won her hitherto marginal West Belfast seat with a sizeable majority. Patricia Ford was a committed campaigner for equal pay, and Patricia McLaughlin, although less concerned with such issues generally, supported Barbara Castle's campaign for the abolition of turnstiles in women's toilets. However, the Women's Orange Lodge established at Westminster during these years presumably had a fairly small membership; Patricia Ford was later expelled from the Lodge for attending a wedding at the Brompton Oratory.

Megan Lloyd George, who had first been elected in 1929, continued to be elected in the early fifties as a Liberal, but lost her seat and later defected to Labour. She was then elected in a by-election in 1957. She continued to hold her seat well into the next decade.

# Women Elected to Parliament in the 1950s

The four general elections of the nineteen fifties saw thirty-six women MPs elected, of whom nineteen went to parliament for the first time. The overall number of women in the House remained low, with the high point – twenty-six women – being reached in 1959. For the remainder of the decade the level remained below the 1945 high of twenty-four.

Women in this list who had been members of previous parliaments are indicated by an asterisk, and it includes women who won seats at by-elections.

|  | Party | Constituency | Elected in |
|---|---|---|---|
| Alice Bacon* | Lab | Leeds North East, Leeds South East | 1950, 1951, 1955, 1959 |
| Bessie Braddock* | Lab | Liverpool Exchange | 1950, 1951, 1955, 1959 |
| Elaine Burton | Lab | Coventry South | 1950, 1951, 1955, 1959 |
| Joyce Butler | Lab | Wood Green | 1955, 1959 |
| Barbara Castle* | Lab | Blackburn | 1950, 1951, 1955, 1959 |
| Freda Corbet* | Lab | Camberwell North West | 1950, 1951, 1955, 1959 |
| Alice Cullen* | Lab | Glasgow Gorbals | 1950, 1951, 1955, 1959 |
| Frances, Viscountess Davidson* | Con | Hemel Hempstead | 1950, 1951, 1955 |
| Evelyn Emmett | Con | East Grinstead | 1955, 1959 |
| Patricia Ford | Unionist | North Down | 1953 (by-election) |
| Muriel, Lady Gammans | Con | Hornsey | 1957 (by-election), 1959 |
| Caroline Ganley* | Lab | Battersea South | 1950 |
| Barbara Gould* | Lab | Hendon North | 1950 |
| Betty Harvie Anderson | Con | Renfrewshire East | 1959 |
| Margaret Herbison* | Lab | Lanarkshire North | 1950, 1951, 1955, 1959 |

# A Great Act of Justice

*Women Elected in the 1950s (cont'd)*

| | | | |
|---|---|---|---|
| Eveline Hill | Con | Manchester Wythenshawe | 1950, 1951, 1955, 1959 |
| Patricia Hornsby-Smith | Con | Chislehurst | 1950, 1951, 1955, 1959 |
| Florence Horsbrugh | Con | Manchester Moss Side | 1950, 1951, 1955, 1959 |
| Lena Jeger | Lab | Holborn & St Pancras | 1953 (by-election), 1955 |
| Jennie Lee* | Lab | Cannock | 1950, 1951, 1955, 1959 |
| Megan Lloyd-George* | Lib/Lab | Anglesey/Carmarthen | 1950, 1957 (by-election), 1959 |
| Jean Mann* | Lab | Coatbridge | 1950, 1951, 1955 |
| Mary McAlister | Lab | Glasgow Kelvingrove | 1957 (by-election) |
| Patricia McLaughlin | Unionist | West Belfast | 1955, 1959 |
| Lucy Middleton* | Lab | Plymouth Sutton | 1950 |
| Edith Pitt | Con | Birmingham Edgbaston | 1953 (by-election), 1955, 1959 |
| Mervyn Pike | Con | Melton | 1956 (by-election), 1959 |
| Dorothy Rees | Lab | Barry | 1950 |
| Harriet Slater | Lab | Stoke-on-Trent | 1953 (by-election), 1955, 1959 |
| Edith Summerskill* | Lab | Fulham West | 1950, 1951, 1955, 1959 |
| Margaret Thatcher | Con | Finchley | 1959 |
| Lady Tweedsmuir* | Con | Aberdeen South | 1950, 1951, 1955, 1959 |
| Joan Vickers | Con | Plymouth Devonport | 1955, 1959 |
| Irene Ward | Con | Tynemouth | 1950, 1951, 1955, 1959 |
| Eirene White | Lab | Flintshire East | 1950, 1951, 1955, 1959 |

## The Flapper Election and After

# Eveline Hill

Eveline Hill was one of the first Conservative women MPs to emerge in her own right from a middle or working class background. Born in Manchester in 1898, she was the daughter of a shopkeeping family. After leaving school she entered the family business where she worked until her marriage in 1922.

In 1936 she was elected to Manchester City Council as a Conservative and worked on housing, health and education issues. She also retained her role running the family business, and engaged in a number of voluntary activities. In 1950 she won the seat of Wythenshawe for her party.

In the House of Commons she retained the interests she had had on the City Council in Manchester (of which she remained a member), but she was also one of the very few women in parliament who had practical business experience, and to this she added an interest in women's issues. She campaigned for equal pay in the public services and in 1951 she introduced the Deserted Wives Bill, which, had it been passed, would have provided some element of financial security for women abandoned by their husbands.

This bill was supported by women across the party divide, but since there were very few of them their influence in this or any other matter was negligible. There were only six Conservative women MPs, and the low number of women Members overall became a matter of such concern that four of them wrote to the Times newspaper demanding action. They pointed out that women often fought seats they could not win, and that the number elected bore no relation to the number who stood. They wanted women to be considered 'on their merits', and believed that local constituency associations were prejudiced against them. 'We write this letter,' they said. 'not as feminists, but because we believe that there are many able and distinguished women who could serve their party and the country if given the chance.' [1]

The Conservative Party did take some note of this lobbying, and efforts were made to secure the election of more women candidates. However, the numbers remained negligible, as did the total number of women in parliament, and the number of Conservative women remained (and remains) very low.

Eveline Hill was defeated in the 1964 general election, and died in 1973.

[1] The Times, 7 March 1952

# Edith Pitt

Edith Pitt was born in 1906 in Birmingham into a working class family. Educated at council schools and evening classes, she became an industrial welfare officer in her native city, and developed a considerable reputation for her work on social issues.

Her studies had included politics and economics, and she was politically active from an early age. She was elected as a Conservative councillor in 1941, and took a keen interest in health matters, particularly as they affected women In the 1950 and 1951 general elections she contested unwinnable seats, and then sought selection for a seat she could win.

In 1953 she was adopted to fight Birmingham Edgbaston, but many local members objected to her, not on the grounds of her gender, but of her class, which was considered inappropriate for an area such as Edgbaston. A rival (male, and well-connected) candidate was found, and the ensuing furore caused considerable embarrassment to the Conservative Party, which at the time was endeavouring to increase the number of women candidates (and MPs). Eventually, Edith's candidacy was confirmed, and she won the seat in 1955 with an increased majority.

In parliament, she continued her work on social issues, particularly housing and health. However, she was also a great advocate of self-reliance, and this led her to oppose measures which she felt threatened this. She was often used by her party as an example of a 'working class woman Tory', and she herself often played up to this. She soon gained promotion to ministerial rank, first at the Ministry of Pensions and National Insurance, and then at the Ministry of Health. In 1962 she lost office in Macmillan's 'night of the long knives' reshuffle, and returned (as a Dame) to the back benches.

After her sudden death in 1966, her seat at Edgbaston was taken by Jill Knight, who in turn was succeeded by Gisela Stewart for Labour in 1997; hence Edgbaston is one of the few seats to have been represented continuously by women for over half a century. Given that the candidates for both Labour and the Conservative parties will be women at the next general election, this tradition could be continued into the next generation of MPs.

# The Sixties

The decade saw two general elections, with eleven new women MPs being elected and a total of 31 women across the decade. The level of women in the House of Commons reached a record 29 in 1964, falling back again to 26 in 1966.

The nineteen sixties saw much social, political and economic change and upheaval, including the advent of the 'Women's Lib' movement. There were significant advances in women's ability to control their reproductive lives – the contraceptive pill became available in 1961, although at that stage it still had to be paid for. Work opportunities improved, and with them women's social and economic status. Given this, it is perhaps surprising that more women did not enter parliament in these years. However, with the notable exception of Bernadette Devlin, the majority of women MPs were the product of the forties and fifties, and although many of them had a real commitment to women's issues, and one or two – such as Barbara Castle – enjoyed a very high profile, young women neither saw them as role models, nor viewed mainstream politics as a relevant vehicle for their aspirations for change.

Despite this a number of key pieces of legislation passed through parliament. In 1964 the Married Women's Property Act finally gave women full control of their money, and allowed them to keep savings made from the housekeeping. The Abortion Law of 1967 legalised abortion in certain circumstances, and in 1969 the Representation of the People Act lowered the voting age to 18.

The nineteen sixties also saw the first female county court judge (Elizabeth Lane in 1962), and the first woman in space (Valentina Tereschkova in 1963). In 1968 women machinists at Ford Dagenham struck for equal pay, bringing to a head the spate of equal pay strikes which had broken out in the preceding year or so. This led directly to the Equal Pay Act of 1970.

Women elected in this decade included several who subsequently became well-known, including Shirley Williams (1964), Renee Short (1964), Shirley Summerskill (1964) and Winifred Ewing, who, as a Scottish Nationalist, won a famous by-election in 1967. Megan Lloyd-George was elected for the last time in 1964, and her death in 1966 broke the last link with the Flapper Election of 1929. In 1969 Bernadette Devlin became, at the age of 21, the youngest woman MP ever to be elected.

# Women Elected to Parliament in the 1960s

The two general elections of the nineteen sixties saw thirty women MPs elected; nine of these were new. In 1964 a new high of twenty-seven women (5% of the House of Commons) was reached, but this fell back to twenty-six in 1966.

Women in this list who had been members of previous parliaments are indicated by an asterisk, and it includes women who won seats at by-elections.

| | Party | Constituency | Elected in |
|---|---|---|---|
| Alice Bacon* | Lab | Leeds South East | 1964, 1966 |
| Bessie Braddock* | Lab | Liverpool Exchange | 1964, 1966 |
| Joyce Butler* | Lab | Wood Green | 1964, 1966 |
| Barbara Castle* | Lab | Blackburn | 1964, 1966 |
| Freda Corbet* | Lab | Peckham | 1964, 1966 |
| Alice Cullen* | Lab | Glasgow Gorbals | 1964, 1966 |
| Bernadette Devlin | Ind Unity | Mid Ulster | 1969 (by-election) |
| Gwyneth Dunwoody | Lab | Crewe & Nantwich | 1966 |
| Winifred Ewing | SNP | Hamilton, Moray & Nairn | 1967 (by-election) |
| Muriel, Lady Gammans* | Con | Hornsey | 1964 |
| Judith Hart* | Lab | Lanark | 1964, 1966 |
| Betty Harvie Anderson* | Con | Renfrewshire East | 1964, 1966 |
| Margaret Herbison* | Lab | Lanarkshire North | 1964, 1966 |
| Patricia Hornsby-Smith* | Con | Chislehurst | 1964 |
| Lena Jeger* | Lab | Holborn & St Pancras | 1964, 1966 |
| Anne Kerr | Lab | Rochester & Chatham | 1964, 1966 |
| Jill Knight | Con | Birmingham Edgbaston | 1966 |
| Jennie Lee* | Lab | Cannock | 1964, 1966 |
| Joan Lestor | Lab | Eton & Slough | Lab |
| Megan Lloyd-George* | Lab | Carmarthen | 1964 |
| Margaret McKay | Lab | Clapham | 1964, 1966 |
| Edith Pitt* | Con | Birmingham Edgbaston | 1964 |
| Mervyn Pike* | Con | Melton | 1964, 1966 |

*Women Elected in the 1960s (cont'd)*

| | | | |
|---|---|---|---|
| Joan Quennell | Con | Petersfield | 1960 (by-election), 1964, 1966 |
| Renee Short | Lab | Wolverhampton North East | 1964, 1966 |
| Harriet Slater* | Lab | Stoke-on-Trent | 1964 |
| Shirley Summerskill | Lab | Halifax | 1964, 1966 |
| Margaret Thatcher* | Con | Finchley | 1964, 1966 |
| Lady Tweedsmuir* | Con | Aberdeen South | 1964 |
| Joan Vickers* | Con | Plymouth Devonport | 1964, 1966 |
| Eirene White* | Lab | Flintshire East | 1964, 1966 |
| Shirley Williams | Lab | Hitchen | 1964, 1966 |

A Great Act of Justice

# The Seventies

The nineteen seventies were a period of considerable political upheaval, with, amongst other things, a miners' strike, the three-day week, two general elections in one year, a coalition government between Labour and the Liberals, and the winter of discontent. It culminated in 1979 with the Conservative general election victory and the installation of Margaret Thatcher as the country's first woman Prime Minister.

A total of forty-two women were elected to parliament in the four general elections which took place during this decade. Over half – twenty-two – of them were new to the Commons, and the decade saw the start of the careers of some very high-profile women, including Margaret Beckett and Betty Boothroyd. There were now no women left from the 1929 election, and only two – Barbara Castle and Freda Corbet – who were first elected in 1945.

The number of women in the Commons remained below the 1964 high of twenty-nine throughout the decade, however, and there continued to be no Liberal women at all. In 1979 the number of women fell below twenty for the first time since 1951. Margaret Thatcher is often criticised for not having had enough women in her cabinets, but it perhaps needs to be borne in mind that in 1979 there were only eight Conservative women (including herself) from whom to choose.

It is also worth noting that in the same year there was only one woman – Gwyneth Dunwoody – in the Labour shadow cabinet, despite there being eleven Labour women MPs.

In other respects, the seventies saw a number of advances for women. Two key pieces of legislation were passed – the Equal Pay Act in 1970 and the Sex Discrimination Act in 1975. The Equal Opportunities Commission was set up in 1976. Oxford colleges were finally all opened to women in 1972, and women were allowed onto the floor of the Stock Exchange in 1973. In 1976 the Domestic Violence Act was passed, and women were at last able to get court orders to protect them from abusive partners.

The face of politics also changed when, against initial expectations, Margaret Thatcher became the first woman to lead a major British political party in 1975. In the 1979 general election which brought her to power, however, the number of women MPs fell back to nineteen, the lowest level since 1951. As a result, women's representation again became an issue for the women's movement, and the scene was set for the developments of the next decade.

# Women Elected to Parliament in the 1970s

The four general elections of the nineteen-seventies saw forty-two women MPs elected, of whom twenty-three went to parliament for the first time. The high point was reached in the second election of 1974, when twenty-seven women were elected; their number declined to nineteen in 1979.

Women in this list who had been members of previous parliaments are indicated by an asterisk, and it includes women who won seats at by-elections.

|  | Party | Constituency | Elected in |
| --- | --- | --- | --- |
| Margaret Bain | SNP | Dunbartonshire East | Oct 1974 |
| Margaret Beckett | Lab | Lincoln | Oct 1974 |
| Betty Boothroyd | Lab | West Bromwich/West Bromwich West | 1973 (by-election), Feb 1974, Oct 1974, 1979 |
| Joyce Butler* | Lab | Wood Green | 1970, Feb 1974, Oct 1974 |
| Barbara Castle* | Lab | Blackburn | 1970, Feb 1974, Oct 1974 |
| Lynda Chalker | Con | Wallasey | Feb 1974, Oct 1974, 1979 |
| Maureen Colquhoun | Lab | Northampton North | Feb 1974, Oct 1974, 1979 |
| Freda Corbet* | Lab | Peckham | 1970 |
| Bernadette Devlin* | Ind Unity | Mid Ulster | 1970 |
| Gwyneth Dunwoody* | Lab | Crewe & Nantwich | Feb 1974, Oct 1974, 1979 |
| Winifred Ewing* | SNP | Hamilton, Moray & Nairn | Feb 1974, Oct 1974, 1979 |
| Sheila Faith | Con | Belper | 1979 |
| Peggy Fenner | Con | Rochester & Chatham | 1970, 1979 |
| Doris Fisher | Lab | Birmingham Ladywood | 1970 |
| Janet Fookes | Con | Merton & Morden/Plymouth Drake | 1970, Feb 1974, Oct 1974, 1979 |
| Joan Hall | Con | Keighley | 1970 |

# A Great Act of Justice

*Women Elected in the 1970s (cont'd)*

| | | | |
|---|---|---|---|
| Judith Hart* | Lab | Lanark | 1970, Feb 1974, Oct 1974, 1979 |
| Betty Harvie Anderson* | Con | Renfrewshire East | 1970, Feb 1974, Oct 1974 |
| Helene Hayman | Lab | Welwyn & Hatfield | Oct 1974 |
| Mary Holt | Con | Preston North | 1970 |
| Patricia Hornsby-Smith* | Con | Chislehurst | 1970 |
| Lena Jeger* | Lab | Holborn & St Pancras South | 1970, Feb 1974, Oct 1974 |
| Elaine Kellett-Bowman | Con | Lancaster | 1970, Feb 1974, Oct 1974, 1979 |
| Jill Knight* | Con | Birmingham Edgbaston | 1970, Feb 1974, Oct 1974, 1979 |
| Joan Lestor* | Lab | Eton & Slough | 1970, Feb 1974, Oct 1974, 1979 |
| Margo MacDonald | SNP | Glasgow Govan | 1973 (by-election)** |
| Joan Maynard | Lab | Sheffield Brightside | Oct 1974, 1979 |
| Oonagh McDonald | Lab | Thurrock | 1976 (by-election), 1979 |
| Millie Miller | Lab | Ilford North | Oct 1974 |
| Constance Monks | Con | Chorley | 1970 |
| Sally Oppenheim | Con | Gloucester | 1970, Feb 1974, Oct 1974, 1979 |
| Mervyn Pike* | Con | Melton | 1970 |
| Joan Quennell* | Con | Joan Quennell* | 1970 |
| Jo Richardson | Lab | Barking | Feb 1974, Oct 1974, 1979 |
| Renee Short* | Lab | Wolverhampton North East | 1970, Feb 1974, Oct 1974, 1979 |
| Shirley Summerskill* | Lab | Halifax | 1970, Feb 1974, Oct 1974, 1979 |
| Ann Taylor | Lab | Bolton West | 1974, 1979 |
| Margaret Thatcher* | Con | Finchley | 1970, Feb 1974, Oct 1974, 1979 |
| Joan Vickers* | Con | Plymouth Devonport | 1970 |

*Women Elected in the 1970s (cont'd)*

| | | | |
|---|---|---|---|
| Shirley Williams* | Lab | Hitchen, Hertford & Stevenage | 1970, Feb 1974, Oct 1974 |
| Audrey Wise | Lab | Coventry South West | Feb 1974, Oct 1974 |
| Sheila Wright | Lab | Birmingham Handsworth | 1979 |

A Great Act of Justice

# Baroness Shirley Williams

Shirley Williams was born in London in 1930, the daughter of a political scientist and the feminist writer Vera Britain. After an education which included Oxford and Columbia University in New York, she became a journalist and then, in 1960, General Secretary of the Fabian Society.

In 1955 she married the philosopher, Bernard Williams.

After standing as an unsuccessful Labour parliamentary candidate twice during the fifties, she was elected in 1964 in Hitchin (later renamed Stevenage). Between 1964 and 1970 she served as a junior minister in several departments, including Labour and Education.

When Labour was returned to office in 1974 she became Secretary of State for Prices and Consumer Protection, and in 1976 James Callaghan appointed her as Secretary of State for Education and Science, where her achievements included the development of the comprehensive education system.

In 1979 Shirley Williams lost her seat as Labour lost power to the incoming government of Margaret Thatcher. In the aftermath of this loss, the Labour Party entered a period of disarray, and, disenchanted with its direction, Shirley Williams and three other prominent members (known as the Gang of Four), resigned from it to form the Social Democratic Party.

In 1981 she stood for her new party in the Crosby by-election and overturned a huge Conservative majority. However, boundary changes in the 1983 election contributed to her losing it again, and her parliamentary career in the Commons came to an end.

During the 1980s she continued to work on both key policy issues and the development of first the Social Democratic and then the Liberal Democrat parties. In 1987 she remarried and moved to America, where she became a professor of Elective Politics at Harvard.

She was made a baroness in 1993, and in 1997 became the Liberal Democrat spokesperson on foreign affairs in the House of Lords. Between 2001 and 2004 she was the Liberal Democrat leader in the Lords.

Baroness Williams continues to be active in the fields which interest her, including international issues and nuclear disarmament.

# Bernadette Devlin (McAliskey)

Born in 1947 in Cookstown, County Tyrone, Bernadette Devlin was orphaned by the age of eighteen. Despite this, she gained a place to study psychology at Queen's University, Belfast, where she became involved with People's Democracy, a civil rights organization led by students.

In 1969 she was elected as the MP for Mid-Ulster in a by-election, and, unlike other nationalist MPs, took her seat on the grounds that she would be able to speak up for both her constituents and the catholic population. At 21 she was – and remains – the youngest woman ever elected.

However, her participation in the Battle of the Bogside in the same year made her both notorious as well as famous, and on her return from a visit to the United Nations in New York she was arrested and served a short prison sentence for incitement to riot.

She was re-elected in 1970 and continued to campaign for civil rights. In 1972 she was a witness to the events of Bloody Sunday in Derry. She was not allowed to speak on the matter in the Commons, and was suspended for assaulting the Home Secretary, Reginald Maudling when he claimed that the British Army had acted in self-defence.

In 1973 she married Michael McAliskey, and lost her seat in 1974. She continued to be active in republican and civil rights politics and campaigns, acting as a spokesperson for the Smash H-Block campaign and the 1981 Hunger Strike. In 1979 she stood unsuccessfully for the European Parliament.

In 1981 she and her husband survived a UDA assassination attempt, and the following year she stood for the Dáil but was not elected. During the nineties she became increasingly marginalised in Irish politics, being critical of the Good Friday Agreement, and opposing Sinn Fein's involvement in government. However, she remains an interesting and, for some, talismanic character, and at the time of her election to parliament represented something strikingly different from the political norm.

# Margaret Beckett

Margaret Beckett was born in Manchester in 1943, and, after education at a local high school, took a degree in metallurgy from Manchester University.

She trained as an engineer, but quickly became involved in Labour politics. In 1973 she fought Lincoln at the by-election won by Dick Taverne, winning the seat when she stood again the following year. At 30, she was one of the younger MPs, and was one of only ten new women entering parliament in the two general elections held in 1974.

She served in various junior government positions before losing her seat in 1979, the year in which she also married Leo Beckett. In 1983 she returned to the Commons as the MP for Derby South, which she continues to represent.

During the 1980s she served in a number of shadow front bench positions, and in 1992 she became the first woman deputy leader of the Party when John Smith became leader; this began a series of firsts stretching into the next century.

In 1994, on John Smith's death, she served as caretaker leader whilst the election for leader – in which she also stood – was held. She was defeated and remains the only woman to have led the Labour Party to date.

She became shadow Health Secretary, and, when Labour took power in 1997, she was appointed as the first woman President of the Board of Trade and Secretary of State for Trade and Industry. She then became Leader of the House and was responsible for steering the first phase of the modernisation of the way in which the House of Commons conducted its business. In 2001 she went to Environment, Food and Rural Affairs, in 2006 becoming the first woman Foreign Secretary.

In 2007, Margaret Beckett returned to the back benches, but in 2008 she rejoined the government as the Housing Minister. In 2009 she returned again to the back benches.

Margaret Beckett has achieved a notable number of firsts for women, and remains one of the most experienced and respected members of the House.

# Breaking New Barriers by Baroness Joyce Gould

*Joyce Gould is a life peer of the House of Lords, and has been Deputy Speaker since 2002. She chairs the Women's National Commission and is involved with many other campaigns and organizations connected with women's rights, interests and health. She holds Doctorates from two universities, and was the first Honorary Fellow of the British Association for Sexual Health. She is also interested in constitutional affairs, race relations, and population and development issues.*

> "Women are not suited to politics for the following reasons. They are often moved by their hearts more than by their heads and the emotional urge which exists in a woman's makeup does not help to good judgement."
>
> Earl of Glasgow. Debate leading to the passage of the Life Peerages Act 1958

**Three months after** the passing of the Act, the first four women Life Peers were announced. Life must have been difficult for them, surrounded by so many hostile men.

It is that very patronising, prejudicial attitude that women generally – and certainly women in politics – have had to battle against and challenge over the years. Women are required to be twice as good as men in order to succeed.

What the Earl of Glasgow expressed was that equal voting rights with men for thirty years had not removed bias and blatant discrimination.

Objections to women as candidates have been many, and mostly spurious. Women were faced with a built-in resistance manifesting itself as: 'There are no suitable women available to stand'; 'We will be risking votes for the party'; 'Women will not vote for a woman'. If a woman did break through and get to a selection meeting, she might be faced with questions, such as at a Conservative Party selection, "You've got three children Mrs Smith. What arrangements have you made?" Or "What does your husband think about you wanting to be an MP?"

The Labour Party was no different. I personally was told after losing a selection by one vote in a marginal seat in Yorkshire "You made the best speech but you look too fragile to take on the task". What he really meant was he did not want a woman candidate.

Women in both major parties have argued the case for more women MPs.

In 1971 the Labour Party National Executive Committee [NEC] communicated this to constituencies and trades unions but with little success. Conservative women felt that they were better at promoting women into Parliament, demonstrated by Margaret Thatcher as the first woman parliamentary party leader and Prime Minister. The Labour Party looked more male in appearance and attitude because of its links with the trades unions, and was personified as a northern male with cloth cap, pipe and a pint. But in reality in all general elections from 1959 the Labour Party has fielded more women candidates, albeit in disgracefully low numbers.

The lack of women candidates did not however preclude a great deal of activity by Labour and Conservative women. The two major parties had powerful, active and forthright women's organizations. Both accepted that Britain was run to the advantage of men but the difference lay in the nature of their political agenda on women's place in society.

Conservative women continued to place the home at the centre of economic, cultural and political objectives whilst Labour women were challenging how to break into that lifestyle designed for men by men.

This was the age of 'women's liberation': of the battered wife; of the campaign for equal pay; legal abortion; the introduction of the pill; bringing women the chance of economic freedom; and of divorce reform – the Casanova's Charter.

The dilemma for Conservative women was how to achieve a balance between their commitment to the home as a private domain, and what was desirable in this new environment. So the role of women in the home came under scrutiny. Their more modern image began to take shape showing greater diversity of view.

This, however, did not prevent Patrick Jenkin, as (Conservative) Opposition Social Services spokesperson, saying, as late as 1977, and much quoted since:

"Quite frankly I don't think mothers have the same right to work as fathers do. If the good Lord had intended us to have equal rights to go out to work he wouldn't have created men and women. These are biological facts."

The question is whether he was supported by the leaders of the women's organizations within the Conservative Party.

But even prior to 1977, the return of a Labour Government showed that little had changed in their instinctive approach to the changing society.

For instance, at the Conservative Women's Conference in 1968, a motion was moved that 'this conference charges the Socialist Government with encouraging more degeneration through legislation such as the Abortion Act'.

# The Flapper Election and After

And there were many other examples of hard hitting attacks by women Conservatives on the 'permissive lifestyle' of the 1960s and 1970s.

At the same time, at the Women's Conferences, Labour women were pushing for equal pay, equal opportunities and better training facilities and persuaded the NEC to set up a study group to investigate the extent of discrimination against women. The study group recommended policies to enable women to achieve equal rights and ultimately we saw the 1970 Equal Pay Act, the 1974 Government White Paper *Equality for Women*, and the Sex Discrimination Act 1975.

It is unknown whether these major achievements would have been promoted without the efforts of the Labour women's organization and its annual conferences, but it seems unlikely.

During her administration, Margaret Thatcher made no attempt to negate these important pieces of legislation. However, she made her view clear in 1975, with:

"... there is far less general desire for equality (as opposed to equity) in Britain than is often claimed ... the pursuit of equality is a mirage".

During her time as Prime Minister, women's roles returned to the home and to a dependency on men.

Yet in spite of the strength of both women's organizations, both Labour and Conservative Parties questioned the need for a separate women's organization.

Elizabeth Hodder, in her book *'Hats off! to Conservative women'* (1990) recalls that on occasions throughout sixty Women's Conferences, doubts have been cast on holding conferences specifically for women. It has been argued that the very existence of a separate women's movement breeds watchfulness and factions rather than solidarity.

The 1968 Labour Party Conference considered a report on Party Organization – the Simpson Report – which recommended changing the structure of the women's organization and controversially abolishing the five places reserved for women on the NEC. In the words of Walter Simpson -

"it was an anachronism, out of time and out of place ... it is a condescension to the women in our Party."

Before the debate, I had been summoned by the much-feared but dynamic National Agent Sarah Barker and told that as the Yorkshire representative on the National Labour Women's Committee I should go to the rostrum and oppose the proposal, and I did.

Ironically, the Report acknowledged that equality had not been achieved, yet in a remarkably inconsistent manner made its proposals as if women had already achieved the euphoric state of equality. No vote was taken, as the NEC had still to consider the Report. The women in the Party ensured this proposal was not heard again for many years.

# A Great Act of Justice

As we reached the end of the 20th century it was a sad indictment that it needed (in 2001) legislation to allow political parties to take positive action to increase the number of women candidates for parliament.

Still, one wonders what the Earl of Glasgow's reaction would be today – with a woman Lord Speaker in the Lords; women as Leader of the House in both Houses; the two most senior Law Officer posts (Attorney General and Solicitor General) held by women, and roughly 30% of Ministerial posts held by women.

However, women continue to be in a minority in Parliament and in public life. We still need to see more women in influential and decision making roles, not least at the centre of power, in Parliament.

# The Eighties

The nineteen eighties in British politics are generally seen as synonymous with the premiership of Margaret Thatcher, the first (and, to date, the only) woman Prime Minister.

The whole decade was a period of substantial change, with opinion still divided on the merits or otherwise of many events. The 1984 miners' strike remains a talismanic event for both right and left, but others – the Falklands war, the dismantling and sale of nationalised industries and women's peace camp at Greenham Common, to name but three – were also highly influential.

In 1981, following what they perceived as a leftwards shift in the Labour Party, Shirley Williams and three other senior members (known as the Gang of Four) left it to form the Social Democratic Party (the SDP). This led to congestion in the middle ground, which eventually resolved itself when the SDP and the Liberals merged in 1988 to become the SLDP, and then, a year later, the Liberal Democrats.

A total of fifty-one women were elected to parliament at the two elections – 1983 and 1987 – during the decade. Thirty-one of these were new parliamentarians. In 1987, Diane Abbott became the first black woman MP, and Ray Michie became the first Liberal MP for a generation. In the same election, the number of women MPs reached forty-one – a high point of 6% of the House of Commons. This represented a massive increase from the twenty-three women elected in 1983, and was at least in part due to increased pressure from women and women's groups as the decade went on.

The establishment in 1980 of the 300 Club, which worked across party lines for equal representation, signalled a renewed campaign to get more women elected, and over the first part of the decade this filtered through into the mainstream parties, particularly Labour. Although good intentions tended to outrun performance by some distance, the number of Labour women MPs more than doubled from ten in 1983 to twenty-one in 1987.

There were also a number of other firsts for women. Baroness Young was the first woman to lead the House of Lords in 1981, and in 1984 Brenda Dean became general secretary of the print union SOGAT and the first woman to lead an industrial trade union. In 1988, Dame Elizabeth Butler-Sloss became the first female law lord.

Other developments included amendments to both the Equal Pay and the Sex Discrimination Acts, the former introducing the concept of equal pay for work of equal value, and the latter allowing women both to retire at the same age as men and to work night shifts.

# A Great Act of Justice

In 1984 Liechtenstein finally enfranchised women, making it the last country in Europe to do so. At the time of writing (November 2009), 6 (24%) of their 25 MPs are women.

# Women Elected to Parliament in the 1980s

There were two General Elections in this decade – 1983 and 1987. A total of 51 women were elected, of whom thirty-one were first-timers.

Women in this list who had been members of previous parliaments are indicated by an asterisk, and it includes women who won seats at by-elections.

|  | Party | Constituency | Elected in |
|---|---|---|---|
| Diane Abbott | Lab | Hackney North & Stoke Newington | 1987 |
| Hilary Armstrong | Lab | Durham North West | 1987 |
| Rosie Barnes | SDP | Greenwich | 1987 |
| Margaret Beckett* | Lab | Derby South | 1983, 1987 |
| Betty Boothroyd* | Lab | West Bromwich/West Bromwich West | 1983, 1987 |
| Virginia Bottomley | Con | Surrey South West | 1984 (by-election), 1987 |
| Lynda Chalker* | Con | Wallasey | 1983, 1987 |
| Ann Clwyd | Lab | Cynon Valley | 1984 (by-election), 1987 |
| Edwina Currie | Con | Derbyshire South | 1983, 1987 |
| Gwyneth Dunwoody* | Lab | Crewe & Nantwich | 1983, 1987 |
| Margaret Ewing* (formerly Bain) | SNP | Moray | 1987 |
| Peggy Fenner* | Con | Medway | 1983, 1987 |
| Janet Fookes* | Con | Plymouth Drake | 1983, 1987 |
| Maria Fyfe | Lab | Glasgow Maryhill | 1987 |
| Llin Golding | Lab | Newcastle-under-Lyme | 1986 (by-election), 1987 |
| Mildred Gordon | Lab | Bow & Poplar | 1987 |
| Teresa Gorman | Con | Billericay | 1987 |
| Harriet Harman | Lab | Camberwell & Peckham | 1982 (by-election), 1983, 1987 |
| Judith Hart* | Lab | Lanark | 1983 |

## *Women Elected in the 1980s (cont'd)*

| | | | |
|---|---|---|---|
| Maureen Hicks | Con | Wolverhampton North East | 1987 |
| Kate Hoey | Lab | Vauxhall | 1989 (by-election) |
| Elaine Kellett-Bowman* | Con | Lancaster | 1983, 1987 |
| Jill Knight* | Con | Birmingham Edgbaston | 1983, 1987 |
| Joan Lestor* | Lab | Eccles | 1987 |
| Alice Mahon | Lab | Halifax | 1987 |
| Joan Maynard* | Lab | Sheffield Brightside | 1983 |
| Anna McCurley | Con | Renfrew West & Invereclyde | 1983 |
| Oonagh McDonald* | Lab | Thurrock | 1983 |
| Helen McElhone | Lab | Glasgow Queen's Park | 1982 (by-election) |
| Ray Michie | Lib, SDLP | Argyll & Bute | 1987 |
| Mo Mowlam | Lab | Redcar | 1987 |
| Emma Nicholson | Con | Devon West & Torridge | 1987 |
| Sally Oppenheim* | Con | Gloucester | 1983 |
| Elizabeth Peacock | Con | Batley & Spen | 1983, 1987 |
| Dawn Primarolo | Lab | Bristol South | 1987 |
| Joyce Quin | Lab | Gateshead East & Washington West | 1987 |
| Jo Richardson* | Lab | Barking | 1983, 1987 |
| Marion Roe | Con | Broxbourne | 1983, 1987 |
| Joan Ruddock | Lab | Lewisham Deptford | 1987 |
| Angela Rumbold | Con | Mitcham & Mordern | 1982 (by-election), 1983, 1987 |
| Elizabeth Shields | Lib | Ryedale | 1986 (by-election) |
| Gillian Shepherd | Con | Norfolk North West | 1987 |
| Clare Short | Lab | Birmingham Ladywood | 1983, 1987 |
| Renee Short* | Lab | Wolverhampton North East | 1983 |

*Women Elected in the 1980s (cont'd)*

| | | | |
|---|---|---|---|
| Ann Taylor* | Lab | Dewsbury | 1987 |
| Margaret Thatcher* | Con | Finchley | 1983, 1987 |
| Joan Walley | Lab | Stoke-on-Trent North | 1987 |
| Ann Widdecombe | Con | Maidstone & the Weald | 1987 |
| Ann Winterton | Con | Congleton | 1983, 1987 |
| Shirley Williams* | SDP | Crosby | 1981 (by-election) |
| Audrey Wise* | Lab | Preston | 1987 |

# A Great Act of Justice

# Margaret Thatcher

Britain's first woman Prime Minister was born in Grantham in 1925 and was educated at the local grammar school before taking a degree in chemistry at Somerville College, Oxford.

She was engaged in politics from an early age, serving as President of the Oxford University Conservative Association. She continued her political activities after she left university, first standing as a candidate at the age of 25 in Dartford.

After university she trained as a tax lawyer, marrying Denis Thatcher in 1951 and having twins in 1953. In 1959 she was elected to parliament for Finchley, which she represented throughout her parliamentary career. At the time of her election she was one of only eleven Conservative women MPs; overall there were just twenty-five women in the House of Commons.

Her political rise was swift; she became a member of the shadow cabinet in 1964 and minister of education in 1970. In 1974, following the Conservative general election defeat, she ousted the incumbent Ted Heath in a leadership election, becoming the first woman to lead a major British political party. In 1979 she became Prime Minister following the Conservative general election victory after the 'winter of discontent'.

During the 1980s her government reformed the way in which trade unions operated, dismantled the nationalised industries and promoted the sale of council houses. She took the country to war in 1982 over the Falkland Islands, and fought a long and bitter campaign against the miners during the strike of 1984/85. She survived the IRA bombing of her hotel in Brighton in 1984. She won three general elections (1979, 1983 and 1987), and introduced the national curriculum, privatisation of parts of the NHS, and the 'poll tax' (or community charge) which provoked particularly fierce opposition.

In 1990 divisions within the Conservative Party finally resulted in a serious leadership challenge, and she was forced to withdraw after failing to secure enough first round votes. She ceased to be prime minister in November 1990, becoming Baroness Thatcher in 1992.

She wrote several books of autobiography, and continued to be active. Following a stroke in 2002 she ceased to accept public speaking engagements, and now lives in retirement.

# Mo Mowlam

Mo Mowlam was born in Watford, the daughter of a post office worker and a telephonist. She was educated both there and in Coventry, and went to Durham University to study social anthropology. She moved to America, where she gained a PhD at Iowa.

In 1979 she returned to the UK and taught at Newcastle University. She became active in the Labour Party there, later moving to South Yorkshire to take up a job at Northern College in Barnsley.

In the 1987 general election she won Redcar, becoming one of a record number of women MPs (forty-one) of whom twenty-one were Labour. She identified herself from the outset with women's issues and interests, and campaigned in particular on low pay issues.

After junior shadow ministerial posts she was promoted to the shadow front bench in 1992 as Labour's spokesperson on women's issues and the citizens' charter, and was appointed shadow Secretary of State for Northern Ireland by Tony Blair in 1994.

In 1995 she married Jon Norton, a merchant banker.

In 1997 she was diagnosed with a brain tumour, but despite this retained her seat in the election and took office in Northern Ireland as the first woman Secretary of State. She was high profile and popular in many – though not all – quarters, and was heavily involved in the negotiations running up to and during the 1998 Good Friday peace deal. Her most controversial act was her visit to the Maze prison, which was regarded by many as a bold move which made a major contribution to getting agreement.

Her time in Northern Ireland turned out to be the high point of her career; she was not offered the major jobs she had hoped for, and instead became Chancellor of the Duchy of Lancaster. In 2001 she retired from parliament, though she continued to write and make public appearances.

She died in 2005. Her long fight against her illness, her outspokenness and her refusal to conform to some of the expected norms made her a popular figure both in and outside politics, and she is remembered for both her personality and her contribution to the peace process in Northern Ireland.

# A Great Act of Justice

# Diane Abbott

Born in 1953 of Jamaican parentage, Diane Abbot was educated at Harrow Grammar School and Newnham College, Cambridge, where she took an MA in History.

She then became a civil servant at the Home Office, but soon moved on to work for the National Council of Civil Liberties (now called Liberty). She later became a freelance journalist before working for TV-AM

In 1982, she became a member of Westminster City Council, and in 1987 was elected as the first black woman member of the House of Commons. At the time there were only three other non-white MPs, and Diane had to deal with issues of race as well as gender. She remained the only black woman MP until 2005, when she was joined by Dawn Butler.

For much of her first decade in parliament she served on the Treasury Select Committee, and, later, the Foreign Affairs Select Committee, but she also took an active interest in other issues, in particular working with fellow black MP Bernie Grant on projects relating to race, the Labour Party and communities. She has been, and remains, an outspoken critic of the way in which her party deals with these issues.

Other interests include international matters as well as education. She took the view that the education system had failed black children, and was particularly critical of fellow Labour MPs who chose to send their children to selective or grant-aided schools. She therefore drew some criticism – and accusations of hypocrisy – when she sent her own child to a private school. Despite this, she has continued to speak out about education, and to campaign for improvements in the way in which it caters for black boys and girls.

She has also, since 2000, campaigned against gun crime, and continues to highlight the problems of young black people in her constituency, as well as campaigning to get more BME women into politics.

She continues to write for various publications, to undertake lecture tours, and to appear regularly on radio and television. She has done more than anyone else to date to raise the profile of black women in politics, and remains a significant figure in the development of political representation in Britain.

# Ray Michie

In 1987 Ray Michie became the first Liberal woman MP since Megan Lloyd George lost her seat in 1951. She was born in Scotland in 1934, the daughter of a Liberal peer, and trained in Edinburgh as a speech therapist marrying Dr Iain Michie in 1957.

Her interest in politics had been sparked at an early age by her father, and continued through her early married life, when she gained experience at various elections and by-elections in Scotland. In the late seventies she was selected to fight a seat for the anticipated Scottish Assembly; when this failed to materialise she stood unsuccessfully for a Westminster seat.

In 1987 she was elected as the Liberal MP for Argyll and Bute. Since she was the only Liberal woman MP she almost immediately became their spokesperson on women's issues, campaigning to correct the imbalance on Select Committees and other parliamentary bodies as well as to get more women into parliament.

Her first love, however, was Scotland, and she was a fierce and successful campaigner on the issues that concerned both her and her constituents. These ranged from working to get a public inquiry into the Chinook helicopter accident on the Mull of Kintyre in 1994 to helping crofters to buy their estates, and she remained a firm advocate of devolution. She also campaigned for better health services in remote areas of Scotland as well as for cultural issues such as the preservation of the Gaelic language.

In 2001, Ray Michie stood down from parliament and was subsequently made a life peer. She took the oath in Gaelic and remained an advocate for Scotland and all things Scottish – at one stage she was joint vice chair of the all-party parliamentary group on the whisky industry.

In 2007 she was appointed to the Scottish Broadcasting Commission, set up to investigate the state of television production and broadcasting in Scotland. She was diagnosed with cancer and died in 2008.

Ray Michie was a highly respected parliamentarian who never became part of the less attractive side of the 'Westminster village', and her campaign for more Liberal Democrat women MPs is now finally beginning to bear fruit.

A Great Act of Justice

# Breaking Through on Merit by Rt Hon Baroness Betty Boothroyd OM

*Betty Boothroyd was born in Dewsbury, Yorkshire, in 1929. Elected Labour MP for West Bromwich in 1973 in her fifth attempt to win a seat, she became a whip in Harold Wilson's government in 1974, a member of the European Assembly 1975-76 and rose to prominence as a member of Labour's national executive 1981-87.*

*Her career took a new direction when she joined the Speaker's Panel of senior MPs who chair the committee stage of Bills in 1979. In 1987, she became a deputy Speaker and her election as Speaker made history on 27 April 1992. She retired in 2000 and was made a life peer with the title Baroness Boothroyd of Sandwell.*

*In keeping with tradition as a former Speaker, she sits in the House of Lords as an independent Cross-Bencher. She was Chancellor of the Open University 1994-2007, Patron of the Memorial to the Women of World War Two in Whitehall and was awarded the Order of Merit by the Queen in 2005. Her autobiography, Betty Boothroyd, was published in 2001.*

**The prospect of** my becoming Speaker of the House of Commons presented me with the sort of challenge I had faced before, but never on the scale that confronted me when the House met for the first time after the 1992 general election.

I had faced many selection committees during my many attempts to become an MP and was used to being rejected. I had also encountered prejudice against women who aspire to public office, although I did not expect it on this occasion. All the same, I had no wish to incite it by saying it was a woman's turn to fill the highest office the House could bestow.

The media thought it was but it would have been fatal for me to put the feminist case. Nor did I believe in it. Through all the ups and downs of my career, I never thought I deserved more rights than a man.

Mrs Thatcher took the same line when she told a reporter: "Don't think of me as the first woman in Downing Street. I'm the first chemist in Downing Street – got it?".

I accepted nomination for the Speaker's chair on a clear understanding: "Elect me for what I am – not for what I was born". Mrs Thatcher was married with twins when she became an MP. I was single and childless. Her critics thought she should care for her family. My critics thought I should get one. We both broke through on our merits.

This time, I was well placed. Re-elected Members that packed the chamber that day had already seen me conduct the business of the House during my five years as a Speaker's deputy. Older colleagues had known me as a Backbencher and as a member of Labour's national executive, where I fought to uphold the party's constitution against extremists.

I believe in the rules that make democracy work. Some of the newcomers that day were Labour MPs, the beneficiaries of our struggles to save the party in the 1980s.

My ambition now was to serve Parliament and preserve its integrity. That was the only basis on which I wanted to be judged.

Everything hung on a dozen or so Tories rejecting their party's preferred choice, the genial Peter Brooke, whom I liked and admired. I knew that most of the 20 Tory women Members would vote for him out of loyalty and I respected that. It proved beyond all doubt that women are not the cohesive group feminists would like us to be.

My hopes rested on persuading enough of their male colleagues to close the gap.

Fortunately, my belief that Parliament's rights must be better protected against the executive mattered more to them than my being a woman. So too did my promise that Backbenchers had rights, as well as Ministers, and I would ensure that their voices were heard in debates, whatever their opinions or standing in their own parties.

After four Tory election victories, the House seemed ready to elect the first Speaker in living memory who did not enjoy the government's support. Breaking the centuries-old, male dominance of the Speaker's chair had grabbed the headlines. That was understandable but incidental, as far as I was concerned.

More seriously, my election was a harbinger of John Major's inability to control the House and the difficulties that lay ahead for both of us. When these arose, and the same applied to Tony Blair's government, I expected no allowances for my being a woman and was given none.

None the less, my fearless friend, Gwyneth Dunwoody, raised the flag for women's rights when she spoke in my favour. Ignoring the raised eyebrows on Tory benches, she referred to the continued under-representation of women in the new Parliament. That was too much for Robert Adley, one of my Tory supporters who retorted that my sex was of no consequence to him. That was fine by me.

To my relief, Gwyneth did not point out that 571 women had stood as candidates in the recent general election and only 60 had been elected. That would have irritated the Tories even more. All the same, I decided to dispel any doubts about where I stood. I told the House:

> "Although having a competent woman Speaker may be a good thing, having a bad woman Speaker would be disastrous. It would be a tragedy for this House, it would be bad for the country, and it would be bad for the cause of women everywhere."

I made it clear at the same time that I did not advocate positive discrimination either. Choosing a person for his or her qualities and abilities was my idea of real equality, whatever their sexual, racial or religious differences.

I had a greater majority than I thought possible. I abstained in the division, which left me wanting 326 votes to win. In the event, I got 372, including 73 Tories and eleven Ministers. Unfortunately for Peter Brooke, the Tory whips had left their canvassing too late whereas my friends had worked hard and secured the support of every minority party. Even Northern Ireland's MPs put aside their differences, which particularly pleased me.

I had served a long apprenticeship. I needed all my wits and experience in the next eight years. I am still surprised by the presumption of some women that political careers can be kick-started at any stage in life. Women's advancement in British politics is a story of gradual progress, built on solid success, a strong sense of duty and a willingness to adjust to a different and demanding lifestyle.

If we have not done as well as we might, we have not done badly either. Margaret Thatcher's three election victories are still unrivalled and I became Speaker 15 years before Nancy Pelosi became Speaker of the House of Representatives.

There were just 26 women MPs when I won West Bromwich in 1973 but their drive and determination did not depend on a secret sisterhood or all-women selection lists.

Labour's high tide in the 1997 election produced an inevitable clash of cultures. Many of Labour's 101 women MPs – the so-called "Blair's babes" – were less hardened than my generation. I upset some of them when I ruled against the breast-feeding of infants in committee meetings. Anne Widdecombe, a Tory of the old school, called my critics "dear little souls" who thought I was "too hard on them and caused more than one to burst into tears". Sadly, some lost heart without the prop of all-women selection lists.

Margaret Jay, a life peer in Tony Blair's cabinet, thought the newcomers lacked "the critical mass to change things and make their voices heard as strongly as they should have been". I doubt that. Women have made their way in Parliament against far greater odds and are still doing so. I salute them and was privileged to be among their number.

# The Nineties

1997 was a significant year in politics in at least two respects – not only was there the biggest single increase in the number of women in parliament, but the England Women's Cricket team was also allowed to compete wearing trousers for the first time.

The decade saw two general elections, and the first of these, in 1992, had itself produced a new record of sixty women MPs, with individual parties achieving new highs as well as the House as a whole. There were twenty Conservative women MPs, a level the party has not reached either before or since (there are currently eighteen Conservative women). Labour had thirty-seven women, and the Liberal Democrats three.

However, pressure in the Labour Party was now building up to a considerable degree, and, after the 1992 election, a decision was taken to introduce a positive action policy using all-women shortlists. This was highly contentious, but was implemented in a significant number of selections before an industrial tribunal in Leeds ruled in 1996 that the policy breached employment law.

Despite this, Labour fielded a greatly increased number of women candidates at the next election, although many of them were in marginal seats and others in seats that the party was not expected to win. In the event, the landslide Labour victory of 1997 meant that after it there were 101 Labour women MPs, whilst the Conservatives fell back to thirteen and the Liberal Democrats increased to five.

The 1990s also saw progress in other respects. Women became eligible to be taxed separately in 1990, and in 1994 marital rape became a criminal offence. In 1999, parental leave was extended to both men and women.

There were firsts for individual women, too. In 1991 Stella Rimmington became the first woman head of MI5. The first black woman QC (Patricia Scotland) was appointed in the same year, and a year later Barbara Mills became the first woman Director of Public Prosecutions. In 1992 the first openly gay woman MP – Angela Eagle – was elected. The first women priests were ordained into the Church of England in 1994, and Pauline Clare became the first female Chief Constable in 1995. In 1998 Rosie Boycott was appointed editor of the Independent, the first daily broadsheet to have a woman in the post. In the following year Merkyn Lowther became Chief Cashier at the Bank of England, and thus the first woman to sign banknotes.

# Women Elected to Parliament in the 1990s

There were two General Elections in this decade – 1992 and 1997. A total of 137 women were elected in this decade, of whom 100 were first-timers.

Women in this list who had been members of previous parliaments are indicated by an asterisk, and it includes women who won seats at by-elections.

|  | **Party** | **Constituency** | **Elected in** |
|---|---|---|---|
| Diane Abbott* | Lab | Hackney North & Stoke Newington | 1992, 1997 |
| Irene Adams | Lab | Paisley North | 1990 (by-election), 1992, 1997 |
| Janet Anderson | Lab | Rossendale & Darwen | 1992, 1997 |
| Hilary Armstrong* | Lab | Durham North West | 1992, 1997 |
| Charlotte Atkins | Lab | Staffordshire Moorlands | 1997 |
| Candy Atherton | Lab | Falmouth & Camborne | 1997 |
| Jackie Ballard | LD | Taunton | 1997 |
| Margaret Beckett* | Lab | Derby South | 1992, 1997 |
| Anne Begg | Lab | Aberdeen South | 1997 |
| Elizabeth Blackman | Lab | Erewash | 1997 |
| Hazel Blears | Lab | Salford | 1997 |
| Betty Boothroyd* | Lab | West Bromwich/West Bromwich West | 1992, 1997 |
| Virginia Bottomley | Con | Surrey South West | 1992, 1997 |
| Angela Browning | Con | Tiverton & Honiton | 1992, 1997 |
| Karen Buck | Lab | Regent's Park & Kensington North | 1997 |
| Christine Butler | Lab | Castle Point | 1997 |
| Anne Campbell | Lab | Cambridge | 1992, 1997 |
| Judith Chaplin | Con | Newbury | 1992 |
| Judith Church | Lab | Dagenham | 1994 (by-election), 1997 |
| Helen Clark (formerly Brinton) | Lab | Peterborough | 1997 |

*Women Elected in the 1990s (cont'd)*

| | | | |
|---|---|---|---|
| Lynda Clark | Lab | Edinburgh Pentlands | 1997 |
| Ann Clwyd* | Lab | Cynon Valley | 1992, 1997 |
| Ann Coffey | Lab | Stockport | 1992, 1997 |
| Yvette Cooper | Lab | Pontefract & Castleford | 1997 |
| Jean Corston | Lab | Bristol East | 1992, 1997 |
| Ann Cryer | Lab | Keighley | 1997 |
| Roseanna Cunningham | SNP | Perth | 1995 (by-election), 1997 |
| Edwina Currie* | Con | Derbyshire South | 1992 |
| Claire Curtis-Thomas | Lab | Crosby | 1997 |
| Valerie Davey | Lab | Bristol West | 1997 |
| Janet Dean | Lab | Burton | 1997 |
| Julia Drown | Lab | Swindon South | 1997 |
| Gwyneth Dunwoody* | Lab | Crewe & Nantwich | 1992, 1997 |
| Angela Eagle | Lab | Wallasey | 1992, 1997 |
| Maria Eagle | Lab | Liverpool Gartson | 1997 |
| Louise Ellman | Lab | Liverpool Riverside | 1997 |
| Margaret Ewing* (formerly Bain) | SNP | Moray | 1992, 1997 |
| Peggy Fenner* | Con | Medway | 1992 |
| Lorna Fitzsimons | Lab | Rochdale | 1997 |
| Caroline Flint | Lab | Don Valley | 1997 |
| Barbara Follett | Lab | Stevenage | 1997 |
| Janet Fookes* | Con | Plymouth Drake | 1992 |
| Maria Fyfe* | Lab | Glasgow Maryhill | 1992, 1997 |
| Cheryl Gillan | Con | Chesham & Amersham | 1992, 1997 |
| Linda Gilroy | Lab | Plymouth Sutton | 1997 |
| Llin Golding* | Lab | Newcastle-under-Lyme | 1992, 1997 |
| Eileen Gordon | Lab | Romford | 1997 |
| Mildred Gordon* | Lab | Bow & Poplar | 1992 |
| Teresa Gorman* | Con | Billericay | 1992, 1997 |
| Harriet Harman | Lab | Camberwell & Peckham | 1992, 1997 |

*Women Elected in the 1990s (cont'd)*

| | | | |
|---|---|---|---|
| Sylvia Heal | Lab | Halesowen & Rowley Regis | 1990 (by-election)1997 |
| Patricia Hewitt | Lab | Leicester West | 1997 |
| Margaret Hodge | Lab | Barking | 1994 (by-election), 1997 |
| Kate Hoey | Lab | Vauxhall | 1992, 1997 |
| Beverley Hughes | Lab | Stretford & Urmston | 1997 |
| Joan Humble | Lab | Blackpool North & Fleetwood | 1997 |
| Glenda Jackson | Lab | Hampstead & Highgate | 1992, 1997 |
| Helen Jackson | Lab | Sheffield Hillsborough | 1992, 1997 |
| Melanie Johnson | Lab | Welwyn Hatfield | 1997 |
| Fiona Jones | Lab | Newark | 1997 |
| Helen Jones | Lab | Warrington North | 1997 |
| Jenny Jones | Lab | Wolverhampton South West | 1997 |
| Lynne Jones | Lab | Birmingham Selly Oak | 1992, 1997 |
| Tessa Jowell | Lab | Dulwich & West Norwood | 1992, 1997 |
| Sally Keeble | Lab | Northampton North | 1997 |
| Ann Keen | Lab | Brentford & Isleworth | 1997 |
| Ruth Kelly | Lab | Bolton West | 1997 |
| Elaine Kellett-Bowman* | Con | Lancaster | 1992 |
| Jane Kennedy | Lab | Liverpool Wavertree | 1992, 1997 |
| Oona King | Lab | Bethnal Green & Bow | 1997 |
| Tess Kingham | Lab | Gloucester | 1997 |
| Julie Kirkbride | Con | Bromsgrove | 1997 |
| Angela Knight | Con | Erewash | 1992 |
| Jill Knight* | Con | Birmingham Edgbaston | 1992 |
| Eleanor Laing | Con | Epping Forest | 1997 |
| Jacqui Lait | Con | Beckenham | 1992, 1997 |
| Jackie Lawrence | Lab | Preseli Pembroke | 1997 |
| Joan Lestor* | Lab | Eccles | 1992 |
| Helen Liddell | Lab | Monklands East, Airdrie & Shotts | 1994 (by-election), 1997 |

# A Great Act of Justice

*Women Elected in the 1990s (cont'd)*

| | | | |
|---|---|---|---|
| Liz Lynne | LD | Rochdale | 1992 |
| Diana Maddock | LD | Christchurch | 1993 (by-election) |
| Fiona Mactaggart | Lab | Slough | 1997 |
| Judy Mallaber | Lab | Amber Valley | 1997 |
| Christine McCafferty | Lab | Calder Valley | 1997 |
| Siobhan McDonagh | Lab | Mitcham & Mordern | 1997 |
| Anne McGuire | Lab | Stirling | 1997 |
| Shona McIsaac | Lab | Cleethorpes | 1997 |
| Anne McIntosh | Con | Vale of York | 1997 |
| Ann McKechin | Lab | Glasgow Maryhill | 1997 |
| Rosemary McKenna | Lab | Cumbernauld & Kilsyth | 1997 |
| Alice Mahon* | Lab | Halifax | 1992, 1997 |
| Olga Maitland | Con | Sutton & Cheam | 1992 |
| Theresa May | Con | Maidenhead | 1997 |
| Gillian Merron | Lab | Lincoln | 1997 |
| Ray Michie* | LD | Argyll & Bute | 1992, 1997 |
| Laura Moffatt | Lab | Crawley | 1997 |
| Margaret Moran | Lab | Luton South | 1997 |
| Julie Morgan | Lab | Cardiff North | 1997 |
| Estelle Morris | Lab | Birmingham Yardley | 1992, 1997 |
| Kali Mountford | Lab | Colne Valley | 1997 |
| Mo Mowlam* | Lab | Redcar | 1992, 1997 |
| Emma Nicholson* | LD/Con | Devon West & Torridge | 1992 |
| Diana Organ | Lab | Forest of Dean | 1997 |
| Sandra Osborne | Lab | Carrick, Cumnock & Doune Valley | 1997 |
| Elizabeth Peacock* | Con | Batley & Spen | 1992 |
| Linda Perham | Lab | Ilford North | 1997 |
| Bridget Prentice* | Lab | Lewisham East | 1992, 1997 |
| Dawn Primarolo* | Lab | Bristol South | 1992, 1997 |
| Joyce Quin* | Lab | Gateshead East & Washington West | 1992, 1997 |

*Women Elected in the 1990s (cont'd)*

| | | | |
|---|---|---|---|
| Jo Richardson* | Lab | Barking | 1992 |
| Barbara Roche | Lab | Hornsey & Wood Green | 1992, 1997 |
| Marion Roe* | Con | Broxbourne | 1992, 1997 |
| Joan Ruddock* | Lab | Lewisham Deptford | 1992, 1997 |
| Angela Rumbold* | Con | Mitcham & Mordern | 1992 |
| Christine Russell | Lab | City of Chester | 1997 |
| Joan Ryan | Lab | Enfield North | 1997 |
| Gillian Shepherd* | Con | Norfolk South West | 1992, 1997 |
| Debra Shipley | Lab | Stourbridge | 1997 |
| Clare Short* | Lab | Birmingham Ladywood | 1992, 1997 |
| Angela Smith | Lab | Basildon | 1997 |
| Geraldine Smith | Lab | Morecambe & Lunesdale | 1997 |
| Jacqui Smith | Lab | Redditch | 1997 |
| Helen Southworth | Lab | Warrington South | 1997 |
| Caroline Spelman | Con | Meriden | 1997 |
| Rachel Squire | Lab | Dunfermline West | 1992, 1997 |
| Phyllis Starkey | Lab | Milton Keynes South West | 1997 |
| Gisela Stuart | Lab | Birmingham Edgbaston | 1997 |
| Ann Taylor* | Lab | Dewsbury | 1992, 1997 |
| Dari Taylor | Lab | Stockton South | 1997 |
| Jenny Tonge | LD | Richmond Park | 1997 |
| Joan Walley* | Lab | Stoke-on-Trent North | 1992, 1997 |
| Claire Ward | Lab | Watford | 1997 |
| Ann Widdecombe* | Con | Maidstone & the Weald | 1992, 1997 |
| Betty Williams | Lab | Conwy | 1997 |
| Ann Winterton* | Con | Congleton | 1992, 1997 |
| Rosie Winterton | Lab | Doncaster Central | 1997 |
| Audrey Wise* | Lab | Preston | 1992, 1997 |

# Women in Government

Women became eligible to hold government office as soon as they were enfranchised, although their progress at that level got off to a very slow start. Individual women were often isolated in male cabinets and government teams, and this continued for many years – in 1968 Harold Wilson was the first prime minister to have two women in the cabinet (Barbara Castle and Judith Hart). The number of women cabinet ministers did not exceed two until Tony Blair appointed five in 1997, and at the time of writing it stands at four out of twenty-three.

The first woman to hold ministerial office at any level was Margaret Bondfield, who was appointed parliamentary secretary at the Ministry of Labour in 1924. She was followed – after the general election of that year – by the Duchess of Atholl, who, as parliamentary secretary at the Board of Education between 1924 and 1929, was the first Conservative woman minister.

When Labour regained power in 1929 Margaret Bondfield became the first woman to join the cabinet (as Minister of Labour), whilst Susan Lawrence became parliamentary secretary at the Ministry of Health.

Between the fall of the Labour government in 1931 and the outbreak of war in 1939 there were no women at all in any kind of ministerial office, but in 1939 Florence Horsburgh became parliamentary secretary at Health, and then, in 1940, was moved to the Ministry of Food in the same capacity. Meanwhile Ellen Wilkinson was briefly a junior minister at Pensions before, between 1940 and 1945, working as joint parliamentary secretary at the Ministry of Home Security. The only other woman minister during this period was Thelma Cazalet-Keir, who was briefly at the Board of Education before the election in 1945.

In 1945 Ellen Wilkinson achieved cabinet rank as Minister of Education, and three other women – Jenny Adamson, Edith Summerskill and Margaret Herbison – held junior posts between then and 1951. Florence Horsburgh became the first Conservative woman cabinet minister in 1953, but in the decade between 1954 and 1964 women were not included in any of the Conservative cabinets, although five – Patricia Hornsby-Smith, Edith Pitt, Mervyn Pike, Margaret Thatcher and Lady Tweedsmuir – held junior posts.

Thus, in the forty-five years between the first woman taking her seat in parliament and the election of the Wilson government in 1964 just fifteen women were members of governments, with only three of them achieving cabinet rank.

Six women took office in 1964; Barbara Castle as a member of the cabinet, and the remainder in junior posts. Barbara Castle remained in the cabinet for the duration of the government, and was joined in 1968 by Judith Hart; altogether ten women were government ministers of one kind or another between 1964 and 1970.

# The Flapper Election and After

The only woman to hold cabinet office in Ted Heath's 1970 government was Margaret Thatcher. Three other women – of whom only Peggy Fenner was a member of the Commons – held lower offices. The Labour government of 1974 returned Barbara Castle to the cabinet, and Shirley Williams was promoted to join her. There were also six women in junior posts.

In 1979, Margaret Thatcher became the first woman prime minister, but throughout her premiership only Baroness Young achieved cabinet rank, and then only for a brief period. A further seventeen women held junior posts at one time or another between 1979 and 1997, with two of them – Virginia Bottomley and Gillian Shepherd – joining the cabinet when John Major took over in 1992.

More than fifty women were members of Tony Blair's various governments between 1997 and 2007. His 1997 cabinet contained five women (Margaret Beckett, Ann Taylor, Mo Mowlam, Clare Short and Harriet Harman), with a further seventeen in junior roles. At various times after that ten more women served as cabinet ministers – Baroness Jay, Estelle Morris, Helen Liddell, Patricia Hewitt, Tessa Jowell, Hilary Armstrong, Hazel Blears, Ruth Kelly, Jacqui Smith and Baroness Amos – and twenty-four served in junior roles. The 1997 cabinet was also the first in which a Minister for Women held cabinet rank.

Gordon Brown's three cabinets since 2007 have contained eight women – Ruth Kelly, Jacqui Smith, Harriet Harman, Hazel Blears, Baroness Ashton, Baroness Royall, Yvette Cooper and Tessa Jowell. Many other women have served in junior posts, with some attending cabinet, and in 2008 Dawn Butler became the first black woman to be appointed to government office.

There are currently women in many – though by no means all – ministerial teams, with those at the Home Office, Transport, International Development and Environment, Food & Rural Affairs being all-male. At the time of writing there are four women cabinet ministers – Harriet Harman, Yvette Cooper, Tessa Jowell and Baroness Royall – and a further twenty-six in junior roles. There are six women in David Cameron's shadow cabinet, and thirteen, many of them peers, in other posts.

Although women have from time to time held office in almost all departments over the years, some ministries tend to recur more than others. Perhaps not surprisingly, women have been most likely to hold the education portfolio (seven), but other patterns are less predictable. Only two women have been Secretary of State for Health, whilst six have held the employment brief in one form or another. Two women have run transport, whilst three have been Chief Whip and three Leader of the House. One woman has been Foreign Secretary, and one Home Secretary, but to date there has been no female Chancellor of the Exchequer and only one woman Prime Minister.

A total of twenty-eight women have held cabinet office since 1918, and of these five have been peers. Thus, in the ninety years since the first woman MP took her seat, just twenty-three elected women have achieved cabinet rank. Clearly, there is room for improvement.

# Women who have served as Cabinet Ministers 1919 – 2009

| In Office | Minister | Portfolio |
| --- | --- | --- |
| 1929-1931 | Margaret Bondfield | Labour |
| 1945-1947 | Ellen Wilkinson | Education |
| 1953-1954 | Florence Horsbrugh | Education |
| 1964-1970<br>1974-1976 | Barbara Castle | Overseas Development<br>Transport, Employment & Productivity |
| 1968-1969 | Judith Hart | Paymaster General |
| 1970-1974<br>1979-1990 | Margaret Thatcher | Education & Science,<br>Prime Minister |
| 1974-1979 | Shirley Williams | Prices & Consumer Protection<br>Education & Science<br>Paymaster General |
| 1982-983 | Baroness Young | Leader of the House of Lords<br>Chancellor of the Duchy of Lancaster<br>Lord Privy Seal |
| 1992-1997 | Virginia Bottomley | Health, National Heritage |
| 1992-1997 | Gillian Shepherd | Employment<br>Agriculture, Fisheries & Food<br>Education & Employment |
| 1997-1998 | Ann Taylor | Leader of the House of Commons<br>Chief Whip |

*Women Cabinet Ministers 1919-2009 (cont'd)*

| | | |
|---|---|---|
| 1997-1998<br>2007- | Harriet Harman | Social Security,<br>Minister for Women<br>Leader of the House of Commons<br>Lord Privy Seal |
| 1997-2001 | Mo Mowlam | Northern Ireland<br>Cabinet Office<br>Chancellor of the Duchy of Lancaster |
| 1997-2003 | Clare Short | International Development |
| 1997-2007 | Margaret Beckett | Trade & Industry<br>Leader of the House of Commons<br>Environment, Food & Rural Affairs<br>Foreign & Commonwealth Office |
| 1998-2001 | Baroness Jay | Lord Privy Seal<br>Leader of the House of Lords<br>Minister for Women |
| 2001-2003 | Helen Liddell | Scotland |
| 2001-2002 | Estelle Morris | Education & Skills |
| 2001-2007 | Patricia Hewitt | Trade & Industry<br>Health |
| 2001-2007<br>2009- | Tessa Jowell | Culture, Media & Sport<br>Cabinet Office<br>Paymaster General |
| 2001-2007 | Hilary Armstrong | Chief Whip<br>Cabinet Office<br>Chancellor of the Duchy of Lancaster |

*Women Cabinet Ministers 1919-2009 (cont'd)*

| | | |
|---|---|---|
| 2003-2007 | Baroness Amos | International Development<br>Leader of the House of Lords |
| 2004-2008 | Ruth Kelly | Cabinet Office<br>Education<br>Community & Local Government<br>Transport |
| 2006-2009 | Hazel Blears | Minister without Portfolio<br>Communities & Local Government |
| 2006-2009 | Jacqui Smith | Home Office |
| 2007-2008 | Baroness Ashton | Leader of the House of Lords<br>Chancellor of the Duchy of Lancaster |
| 2008- | Yvette Cooper | Chief Secretary to the Treasury<br>Work & Pensions |
| 2008- | Baroness Royall | Leader of the House of Lords<br>Chancellor of the Duchy of Lancaster |

# The Twenty-first Century

It might have been expected that, after the significant increase in the number of women MPs in 1997, the first decade of the new millennium would see continued improvement. In fact, this turned out not to be the case. In the 2001 general election there were only ten new women MPs – four Labour, two Liberal Democrats, one Conservative, and three from Northern Ireland, one of whom did not take her seat.

For the 1997 election, the Labour Party had used positive action mechanisms to increase the number of women candidates in winnable seats; this was not the case for the 2001 election. After it, legislation was passed to enable all parties to use positive action if they chose, thus addressing the problem caused by the 1996 Leeds Industrial Tribunal decision.

At the 2005 general election, for which Labour re-instated positive action, thirty-eight new women MPs were successful – twenty-six Labour, six Conservative and six Liberal Democrat. Since then, both the Conservative and Liberal Democrat parties have confirmed their opposition to all-women shortlists, the mechanism used by Labour, but have taken a number of other steps to increase the number of candidates they field in winnable seats. As a result, all three of the main parties will stand increased numbers of women at the next election; it remains to be seen what effect on the overall percentage of women MPs this will have.

In other respects, the decade continued to see landmark firsts for women both in and out of politics. In 2000, the Women's Peace Camp at Greenham Common closed down. A year later Amnesty International appointed its first woman Secretary General, Irene Zubaida Khan, and Clara Furse became the first woman chief executive of the London Stock Exchange. Women began to reach the higher offices of the Church of England, though they were still barred from bishoprics. Baroness Valerie Amos became the first black woman cabinet minister in 2003, Margaret Beckett the first female Foreign Secretary in 2006 and Jacqui Smith the first female Home Secretary in 2007.

In terms of legislation, the Civil Partnership Act of 2005 gave same-sex couples legal rights, and the adoption laws were revised to allow same sex couples to adopt.

The Isle of Man passed its first sex discrimination legislation in 2001, whilst at Oxford, the last all-female college (St Hilda's) decided to accept male students in 2006.

The next general election, which will happen within nine months of this publication, will doubtless bring further changes to the representation of women, and what some of these might be are considered in later sections of this book.

*A Great Act of Justice*

# Women Elected to Parliament in the Twenty-First Century

To date, there have been two general elections in the first decade of the new millennium – 2001 and 2005. A total of 155 women were elected at these elections, of whom 51 were first-timers.

Women in this list who had been members of previous parliaments are indicated by an asterisk, and it includes women who won seats at by-elections.

|  | Party | Constituency | Elected in |
|---|---|---|---|
| Diane Abbott* | Lab | Hackney North & Stoke Newington | 2001, 2005 |
| Irene Adams* | Lab | Paisley North | 2001 |
| Janet Anderson* | Lab | Rossendale & Darwen | 2001, 2005 |
| Hilary Armstrong* | Lab | Durham North West | 2001, 2005 |
| Charlotte Atkins* | Lab | Staffordshire Moorlands | 2001, 2005 |
| Candy Atherton* | Lab | Falmouth & Camborne | 2001 |
| Vera Baird | Lab | Redcar | 2001, 2005 |
| Celia Barlow | Lab | Hove | 2005 |
| Margaret Beckett* | Lab | Derby South | 2001, 2005 |
| Anne Begg* | Lab | Aberdeen South | 2001, 2005 |
| Elizabeth Blackman* | Lab | Erewash | 2001, 2005 |
| Roberta Blackman-Woods | Lab | City of Durham | 2005 |
| Hazel Blears* | Lab | Salford | 2001, 2005 |
| Virginia Bottomley* | Con | Surrey South West | 2001 |
| Annette Brooke | LD | Mid Dorset & Poole North | 2001 |
| Lyn Brown | Lab | West Ham | 2005 |
| Angela Browning* | Con | Tiverton & Honiton | 2001, 2005 |
| Karen Buck* | Lab | Regent's Park & Kensington North | 2001, 2005 |
| Lorely Burt | LD | Solihull | 2005 |
| Dawn Butler | Lab | Brent South | 2005 |
| Patsy Calton | LD | Cheadle | 2001, 2005 |

*Women Elected in the 21st Century (cont'd)*

| | | | |
|---|---|---|---|
| Anne Campbell* | Lab | Cambridge | 2001 |
| Katy Clark | Lab | Ayrshire North & Arran | 2005 |
| Lynda Clark* | Lab | Edinburgh Pentlands | 2001 |
| Ann Clwyd* | Lab | Cynon Valley | 2001, 2005 |
| Ann Coffey* | Lab | Stockport | 2001, 2005 |
| Rosie Cooper | Lab | Lancashire West | 2005 |
| Yvette Cooper* | Lab | Pontefract & Castleford | 2001, 2005 |
| Jean Corston* | Lab | Bristol East | 2001 |
| Mary Creagh | Lab | Wakefield | 2005 |
| Ann Cryer* | Lab | Keighley | 2001, 2005 |
| Claire Curtis-Thomas* | Lab | Crosby | 2001, 2005 |
| Valerie Davey* | Lab | Bristol West | 2001 |
| Janet Dean* | Lab | Burton | 2001, 2005 |
| Nadine Dorries | Con | Mid Bedfordshire | 2005 |
| Julia Drown* | Lab | Swindon South | 2001 |
| Gwyneth Dunwoody* | Lab | Crewe & Nantwich | 2001, 2005 |
| Angela Eagle* | Lab | Wallasey | 2001, 2005 |
| Maria Eagle* | Lab | Liverpool Gartson | 2001, 2005 |
| Louise Ellman* | Lab | Liverpool Riverside | 2001, 2005 |
| Natascha Engel | Lab | Derbyshire North East | 2005 |
| Lynne Featherstone | LD | Hornsey & Wood Green | 2005 |
| Lorna Fitzsimons* | Lab | Rochdale | 2001 |
| Caroline Flint* | Lab | Don Valley | 2001, 2005 |
| Barbara Follett* | Lab | Stevenage | 2001, 2005 |
| Sandra Gidley | LD | Romsey | 2000 (by-election), 2001, 2005 |
| Michelle Gildernew | SF | Fermanagh & South Tyrone | 2001, 2005 |
| Cheryl Gillan* | Con | Chesham & Amersham | 2001, 2005 |
| Linda Gilroy* | Lab | Plymouth Sutton | 2001, 2005 |

# A Great Act of Justice

*Women Elected in the 21st Century (cont'd)*

| | | | |
|---|---|---|---|
| Julia Goldsworthy | LD | Falmouth and Camborne | 2005 |
| Helen Goodman | Lab | Bishop Auckland | 2005 |
| Justine Greening | Con | Putney | 2005 |
| Nia Griffith | Lab | Llanelli | 2005 |
| Harriet Harman* | Lab | Camberwell & Peckham | 2001, 2005 |
| Sylvia Heal* | Lab | Halesowen & Rowley Regis | 2001, 2005 |
| Sylvia Hermon | UUP | North Down | 2001, 2005 |
| Patricia Hewitt* | Lab | Leicester West | 2001, 2005 |
| Meg Hillier | Lab | Hackney South & Shoreditch | 2005 |
| Margaret Hodge* | Lab | Barking | 2001, 2005 |
| Sharon Hodgson | Lab | Gateshead East & Washington West | 2005 |
| Kate Hoey* | Lab | Vauxhall | 2001, 2005 |
| Beverley Hughes* | Lab | Stretford & Urmston | 2001, 2005 |
| Joan Humble* | Lab | Blackpool North & Fleetwood | 2001, 2005 |
| Glenda Jackson* | Lab | Hampstead & Highgate | 2001, 2005 |
| Helen Jackson* | Lab | Sheffield Hillsborough | 2001 |
| Siân James | Lab | Swansea East | 2005 |
| Diana Johnson | Lab | Hull North | 2005 |
| Melanie Johnson* | Lab | Welwyn Hatfield | 2001 |
| Helen Jones* | Lab | Warrington North | 2001, 2005 |
| Lynne Jones* | Lab | Birmingham Selly Oak | 2001, 2005 |
| Tessa Jowell* | Lab | Dulwich & West Norwood | 2001, 2005 |
| Sally Keeble* | Lab | Northampton North | 2001, 2005 |
| Barbara Keeley | Lab | Worsley | 2005 |
| Ann Keen* | Lab | Brentford & Isleworth | 2001, 2005 |
| Ruth Kelly* | Lab | Bolton West | 2001, 2005 |
| Jane Kennedy* | Lab | Liverpool Wavertree | 2001, 2005 |
| Oona King* | Lab | Bethnal Green & Bow | 2001 |

*Women Elected in the 21st Century (cont'd)*

| | | | |
|---|---|---|---|
| Julie Kirkbride* | Con | Bromsgrove | 2001, 2005 |
| Susan Kramer | LD | Richmond Park | 2005 |
| Eleanor Laing* | Con | Epping Forest | 2001, 2005 |
| Jacqui Lait* | Con | Beckenham | 2001, 2005 |
| Jackie Lawrence* | Lab | Preseli Pembroke | 2001 |
| Helen Liddell* | Lab | Monklands East, Airdrie & Shotts | 2001 |
| Fiona Mactaggart* | Lab | Slough | 2001, 2005 |
| Anne Main | Con | St Albans | 2005 |
| Judy Mallaber* | Lab | Amber Valley | 2001, 2005 |
| Christine McCafferty* | Lab | Calder Valley | 2001, 2005 |
| Kerry McCarthy | Lab | Bristol East | 2005 |
| Sarah McCarthy-Fry | Lab | Portsmouth North | 2005 |
| Siobhan McDonagh* | Lab | Mitcham & Mordern | 2001, 2005 |
| Anne McGuire* | Lab | Stirling | 2001, 2005 |
| Shona McIsaac* | Lab | Cleethorpes | 2001, 2005 |
| Anne McIntosh* | Con | Vale of York | 2001, 2005 |
| Ann McKechin* | Lab | Glasgow Maryhill | 2001, 2005 |
| Rosemary McKenna* | Lab | Cumbernauld & Kilsyth | 2001, 2005 |
| Alice Mahon* | Lab | Halifax | 2001 |
| Theresa May* | Con | Maidenhead | 2001, 2005 |
| Gillian Merron* | Lab | Lincoln | 2001, 2005 |
| Maria Miller | Con | Basingstoke | 2005 |
| Anne Milton | Con | Guildford | 2005 |
| Anne Moffat | Lab | East Lothian | 2001, 2005 |
| Laura Moffatt* | Lab | Crawley | 2001, 2005 |
| Madeleine Moon | Lab | Bridgend | 2005 |
| Margaret Moran* | Lab | Luton South | 2001, 2005 |
| Jessica Morden | Lab | Newport East | 2005 |
| Julie Morgan* | Lab | Cardiff North | 2001, 2005 |
| Estelle Morris* | Lab | Birmingham Yardley | 2001 |
| Kali Mountford* | Lab | Colne Valley | 2001, 2005 |
| Meg Munn | Lab | Sheffield Healey | 2001 |

# A Great Act of Justice

*Women Elected in the 21st Century (cont'd)*

| Name | Party | Constituency | Years |
|---|---|---|---|
| Diana Organ* | Lab | Forest of Dean | 2001 |
| Sandra Osborne* | Lab | Carrick, Cumnock & Doune Valley | 2001, 2005 |
| Linda Perham* | Lab | Ilford North | 2001 |
| Anne Picking | Lab | East Lothian | 2001 |
| Bridget Prentice* | Lab | Lewisham East | 2001, 2005 |
| Dawn Primarolo* | Lab | Bristol South | 2001, 2005 |
| Joyce Quin* | Lab | Gateshead East & Washington West | 2001 |
| Iris Robinson | DUP | Strangford | 2001, 2005 |
| Barbara Roche* | Lab | Hornsey & Wood Green | 2001 |
| Marion Roe* | Con | Broxbourne | 2001 |
| Linda Riordan | Lab | Halifax | 2005 |
| Joan Ruddock* | Lab | Lewisham Deptford | 2001, 2005 |
| Christine Russell* | Lab | City of Chester | 2001, 2005 |
| Joan Ryan* | Lab | Enfield North | 2001, 2005 |
| Alison Seabeck | Lab | Plymouth Devonport | 2005 |
| Gillian Shepherd* | Con | Norfolk South West | 2001 |
| Debra Shipley* | Lab | Stourbridge | 2001 |
| Clare Short* | Lab | Birmingham Ladywood | 2001, 2005 |
| Angela Smith* | Lab | Basildon | 2001, 2005 |
| Angela Smith | Lab | Sheffield Hillsborough | 2005 |
| Chloe Smith | Con | Norwich North | 2009 (by-election) |
| Geraldine Smith* | Lab | Morecambe & Lunesdale | 2001, 2005 |
| Jacqui Smith* | Lab | Redditch | 2001, 2005 |
| Anne Snelgrove | Lab | Swindon South | 2005 |
| Helen Southworth* | Lab | Warrington South | 2001, 2005 |
| Caroline Spelman* | Con | Meriden | 2001, 2005 |
| Rachel Squire* | Lab | Dunfermline West | 2001 |
| Phyllis Starkey* | Lab | Milton Keynes South West | 2001, 2005 |

# The Flapper Election and After

*Women Elected in the 21st Century (cont'd)*

| | | | |
|---|---|---|---|
| Gisela Stuart* | Lab | Birmingham Edgbaston | 2001, 2005 |
| Jo Swinson | LD | Dunbartonshire East | 2005 |
| Ann Taylor* | Lab | Dewsbury | 2001 |
| Dari Taylor* | Lab | Stockton South | 2001, 2005 |
| Sarah Teather | LD | Brent East | 2003 (by-election), 2005 |
| Emily Thornberry | Lab | Islington South & Finsbury | 2005 |
| Jenny Tonge* | LD | Richmond Park | 2001 |
| Kitty Usher | Lab | Burnley | 2005 |
| Theresa Villiers | Con | Chipping Barnet | 2005 |
| Joan Walley* | Lab | Stoke-on-Trent North | 2001, 2005 |
| Linda Waltho | Lab | Stourbridge | 2005 |
| Claire Ward* | Lab | Watford | 2001, 2005 |
| Angela Watkinson | Con | Upminster | 2001, 2005 |
| Ann Widdecombe* | Con | Maidstone & the Weald | 2001, 2005 |
| Betty Williams* | Lab | Conwy | 2001, 2005 |
| Jenny Willott | LD | Cardiff Central | 2005 |
| Ann Winterton* | Con | Congleton | 2001, 2005 |
| Rosie Winterton* | Lab | Doncaster Central | 2001, 2005 |

# A Great Act of Justice

# Conservative Women

It is sometimes the case that parties which oppose particular measures find themselves responsible for bringing them in; this was the case with the Conservative Party and both of the major pieces of legislation enfranchising women.[1] However, this did not mean that the party – or, more particularly, its members – approved of women participating in politics, and women seeking selection as Conservative candidates encountered opposition from the outset.

One route which did not draw disapproval was 'inheritance', usually from a husband. Nancy Astor, the first Conservative woman MP, and the first woman to take her seat, stood only when her MP husband was ennobled, and of the four Conservative women elected between 1918 and 1928 three (Nancy Astor, the Countess of Iveagh and Mabel Philipson) took seats over from their husbands.

The 1929 election produced no new Conservative women MPs, but in the nineteen-thirties, when the Conservative Party as a whole did better at the polls, the three elected in the Flapper Election (Astor, Iveagh and the Duchess of Atholl) were joined by eleven others, including Florence Horsbrugh who, after the Second World War, became the first Conservative woman to hold cabinet office.

Conservative women were not exactly encouraged by the party hierarchy to stand as parliamentary candidates, and the Countess of Iveagh's observation that:

> 'I can only speak for the party which I represent, but I think the statement cannot be challenged that though women are politically better organized than men, are politically much more active than men, it is extremely difficult to get a woman candidate adopted in a constituency'[2]

remained true for decades.

The high point of thirteen Conservative women MPs in 1931 was not reached again until 1970, when there were fifteen, and the record number of twenty was not achieved until 1992. There are currently eighteen Conservative women in the House of Commons (6% of a total of 193).

The Conservative Party has traditionally always had very strong women's organizations which were, as the Countess remarked, both well-organized and active, but whose role was not perceived as being to promote the representation of women. These dated back to the foundation of the Ladies Branch of the Primrose League in 1885, but the involvement of women in canvassing and campaigning was by that point already well-established. In 1919 the forerunner of the current

---

[1] The Conservative Home Secretary Sir George Cave was responsible for steering the 1918 Act through the House, and his successor Sir William Joynson-Hicks was responsible for the 1928 Act.
[2] Speaking in the debate on the 1928 Bill

Conservative Women's Organization was established, and held its first conference in 1921; it grew rapidly and maintained high levels of membership eventually becoming the largest women's political organization in Europe.

In 1979 the Conservative Party achieved another notable first for political women when Margaret Thatcher became prime minister. Although the next decade saw slow and steady progress, having a female prime minister did not lead to a significant increase in the number of Conservative women MPs; in 1979 there were eight, in 1983 thirteen, in 1987 seventeen and in 1992 twenty.

In 1997, the number of Conservative women fell back to thirteen, and since then has risen again to its current level. However, it was clear to both the party leadership and individual women that something more concerted needed to be done, and this led to the formation of *women2win*, set up to support women candidates, as well as to a much more proactive approach by the party's leadership. This has had results in terms of the selection of women candidates, and at the next general election more Conservative women will be fielded in seats they can win than ever before.

A Great Act of Justice

# The Conservative Approach by Rt Hon Theresa May MP

*Theresa May is currently the Shadow Secretary of State for Work and Pensions (since 2009) and has been the Shadow Minister for Women (since 2007). From 2002 to 2003 she was the first woman Chairman of the Conservative Party.*

*Having worked in the City before becoming an MP, she has experience of life outside Westminster, but has also been involved in politics at all levels for many years, both as a party worker and, between 1986 and 1994, a local councillor in Merton. She was elected Member of Parliament for Maidenhead in May 1997.*

*Theresa has held several positions within Parliament since 1997. She has been a member of the Shadow Cabinet since 1999, including as Shadow Secretary of State for Education and Employment (1999-2001), Shadow Secretary of State for Transport, Local Government and the Regions (2001-02), Shadow Secretary of State for the Family (2004-05, including Culture, Media and Sport in 2005), and Shadow Leader of the House of Commons (2005-09).*

**Eighty years ago**, women voted in the first General Election with universal suffrage after years of violent struggles and political debate. Since that point, the role of women in politics, business and society has progressed beyond recognition. Now as many women turn out to vote as men, and there are 128 women MPs sitting in Parliament.[1]

In the business world, where eighty years ago they were absent, women have stepped forward. We are now at the point where we can proudly say there are around 620,000 majority women-owned businesses in the UK, generating around £130 billion turnover. And at long last most businesses have realised that employing a woman is not a hindrance but an asset.

Furthermore, eighty years ago only a handful of universities admitted women and now there are more women at university in the UK than men. In all of these spheres

---

[1] Figure as of 2005 General Election

it is noticeable that women have not waited for men to give us rights but have gone out and achieved tremendous progress for ourselves and this is something that should be celebrated.

But despite all of these milestones being reached, have we achieved true equality? I would like to look in particular at the world of politics and the role that women play within the traditional environs of the Houses of Parliament. I think this is a particularly relevant angle as, in many ways, politics has been at the centre of the debate from the beginning. The suffragettes were focusing their efforts on women getting the vote – for these women this was the barometer of what was just, equal and right. Once this was achieved other milestones started to fall; more women started to enter business, the media and education.

Since Nancy Astor, the first female MP to take up her seat, entered the House of Commons in 1919 there have been vast improvements in female representation in Parliament. Indeed, when Margaret Thatcher was returned as the first female Prime Minister in 1979, she did so at a time when women who had been born without any prospect of a vote, were still alive. The achievements of these and other women must not be forgotten and we must be careful they are not taken for granted as people assume that the battle for equality has been won.

Sadly, the statistics show this is far from the case. Indeed, whilst over 50% of the UK population is female, only 19.8% of MPs are women.[2] The pace of change is not fast enough and this is true for all the major political parties. Before 2007, at the rate we were going, it would have taken the Conservative Party four hundred years to achieve equal representation of women within its ranks. However, it would still take over two hundred years at the current rate for Parliament to be comprised of an equal number of men and women.

David Cameron and I are not prepared to wait for that to happen and drastic action has been taken to change attitudes within the Conservative Party now. I firmly believe we should all aspire to a selection process based on the skills of the individual which leads to a fair and diverse Parliament. It is absolutely crucial that our candidates are primarily selected on merit. This is a hugely important job and we need to have the best people in place, regardless of their sex, age, race or any other factor.

It is important to assess people's ability to do the job objectively. That's why the Party introduced a skills analysis for prospective candidates. I also introduced American-style selection 'primaries', which enables the selection of a candidate to be made by a wider group of people in a constituency than just Party members.

Further to this we introduced a priority list that would help promote female candidates by being gender balanced. There are "many very, very good women" on our list of candidates who have not yet been selected and who we want to see as MPs.

[2] Figure as of 2005 General Election

# A Great Act of Justice

David Cameron made clear from the day he was elected as Leader of the Party that he wants to see more women Conservative MPs. We have reached the point where around 30% of our candidates are women, which is a higher proportion than either Labour or the Liberal Democrats fielded in the last general election. Indeed, if the next Parliament sees a Conservative government with a majority of just one, then it is likely nearly sixty women will be sitting on Conservative benches, our highest ever total.

However, this progress is still not enough; as David Cameron has said we need to get more women into politics and we will continue to fight to ensure more female representation.

From January, our party will move to our by-election procedure which means that if any MP stands down, either shortly before that date or after that date, the Party centrally will provide a shortlist of candidates to their association. This is normal practice. It is David Cameron's intention that some of those shortlists will be all-women short lists – as recognition that there are many very, very talented women on our candidates' list who haven't yet been selected.

I am also proud to be co-founder of women2win. This has provided vital support for Conservative women candidates, guiding them through the process and helping to ensure that nearly a third of our selected candidates for the next election are women. It has helped to encourage women to come forward into a successful and dynamic atmosphere where they will be listened to.

So why are we working so hard for fair representation of women who, according to some, make second-rate MPs? This is simply because that argument is false. In my experience, women make excellent MPs. I often say to people who are talking about women in politics and Parliament that they should listen to debates predominantly involving women, because they will hear a different quality to them; different in sentiment, feeling and expression.

Politics has changed. The average person on the streets prioritises health and education as big issues. Questions that matter to women, such as social reform and the welfare state have risen up the political agenda. This is why it is vital we continue to get more women MPs into parliament, so we can keep pace with the new, feminised political agenda.

I disagree with those who say this is a question of political correctness or mere quota-filling. This is not about being politically correct, but politically effective. I do not believe it is necessary for British society to be directly reflected in Parliament for it to be fairly represented. It is important not to confuse the ability of Parliament to reflect society with its ability to represent society.

However, I do believe that Parliament should be drawn from the widest pool of talent in order to ensure better decision making. I am pleased to see that measures the Conservative Party are taking now will have an effect on numbers of women Conservative MPs whilst laying the foundations for a fair and representative Parliament in the future.

# Labour Women

The Labour Party had, generally speaking, supported the enfranchisement of women, but it did so within the context of its wider commitment to socialism, and the need to reconcile its wider political objectives with its commitment to women is a thread which has run through its relationship with its women members from that point to this.

In 1906, when the first Labour MPs were elected, the new all-male Parliamentary Labour Party (PLP) included women's suffrage amongst its priorities. In the same year the Women's Labour League was formed, accepting into membership a wide range of women from the Labour movement as a whole. In 1911 the formidable Marion Phillips became the League's Secretary and edited the *Labour Woman*, an influential publication, for the next twenty years.

In 1918 the Women's Labour League was dissolved, and women were admitted as individual members of the Labour Party, though in separate Women's Sections and in a subordinate role. Marion Phillips, who was appointed as the party's first Women's Officer, was of the view that this would enable women – for generations excluded from politics – to educate themselves and prepare themselves for office, and saw no contradiction between the structure she was instrumental in establishing and her undoubted drive to get Labour women into parliament.

The party as a whole also took the view that, until the interests of the working class had been secured those of women must wait, and many – then as now – saw feminism as a middle class concern which had little relevance for working class women. As a result, the progress of women was slow, and women found it difficult from the start to get selected as candidates for seats that were anything other than marginal.

The first Labour women MPs (Margaret Bondfield, Susan Lawrence and Dorothy Jewson) were elected in 1923, but two of them lost their seats in the following year. In 1929 there were nine Labour women MPs, but all of them lost in 1931. The number of Labour women MPs fluctuated wildly in the ensuing decades, rising from one in 1935 to twenty-one in 1945, and falling again to ten in 1970 and 1983.

In the nineteen eighties, however, women members inside the Labour Party, working in some cases with feminists outside it, began to make a concerted effort to get more of their number selected in seats they could win. As a result, the number of women elected more than doubled between 1983 and 1987, and rose to a record thirty-seven in 1992. This reflected not only a more proactive approach on the part of the party itself, but also the establishment in 1988 of the Labour Women's Network, which – separately from the party – provided training and mentoring for women candidates.

Despite the success of 1992, pressure for a more effective approach continued, and for the 1997 round of candidate selections the party decided, amidst much controversy, to implement a policy known as all-women shortlists (AWS), under which half of all winnable seats would have to select women candidates.

In 1996, this policy was successfully challenged at an Industrial Tribunal in Leeds, and selections for seats after that were made from mixed shortlists.

Despite this, and partly because the scale of the Labour victory saw many women in highly marginal seats elected, 101 Labour women entered parliament in 1997.

All Labour candidates for the 2001 campaign were selected from mixed shortlists, and at the subsequent general election the number of women Labour MPs fell to 95, rising again to 98 (30% of the PLP) in 2005 following the reinstatement of AWS.

AWS is also being used to select candidates for the next election, and it is therefore probable that Labour will field a high number of women candidates in addition to the women MPs defending their seats. However, women MPs generally tend to be in more marginal seats, and it remains to be seen whether or not the Labour Party can continue progress towards its target of half of its MPs being women.

# Leading the Way
# by Maria Eagle MP

*Maria Eagle is the Parliamentary Secretary for Equalities and the Parliamentary Undersecretary of State at the Ministry of Justice. She is the Labour MP for Liverpool Garston.*

*She was born in Yorkshire, and, after taking a degree from Pembroke College, Oxford, became a solicitor. She has experience of both the voluntary sector and the legal profession, and entered parliament in 1997. She entered government after the 2001 election, and has served at various ministries including Work & Pensions, Health and Northern Ireland.*

*Maria Eagle has been involved in campaigns to increase the number of Labour women for some years, and continues to work for the broadening of the base of representation through her work as Parliamentary Secretary for Equalities.*

**Eighty years have** passed since the 1929 General Election – otherwise known as the Flapper Election – the first at which all women and men over the age of 21 were able to vote. Nineteen General Elections later, and today, not only do women continue to benefit from both the right and opportunity to vote, but their participation in public and political life has also improved dramatically.

The number of women MPs continues to increase with women currently making up nearly 20% of the House of Commons compared to 9% before 1997. Much of this change has come about because of action that the UK Government has introduced to allow political parties to use positive measures towards women's increased participation.

Ensuring more women have the opportunity and support to take up key decision-making positions is critical. Achieving fair representation is not only just, it is symbolic, ensuring decision-makers are seen as effective role models and as truly representative of their electors. This helps to ensure the political process is seen by the public as fresh, modern and in touch with the communities and places it serves. Research published by the Electoral Commission suggests that having more women elected representatives actually encourages greater participation rates amongst women more generally.

Representation is also a question of ensuring a higher quality of decision-making by reflecting the greater diversity of experience of those making the decisions. Women in Parliament and wider decision-making positions tend to have a better understanding of what women need and want, and can therefore better represent their views and those of their families. We only have to look at the policies introduced since 1997 which reflect this: increase in childcare, introduction of flexible working rights and legislation to tackle domestic violence, forced marriage etc.

Since 1997 a number of significant firsts for parliamentary women have been achieved. In that year the first black women peers – Baroness Amos and Baroness Scotland – were appointed, with Baroness Amos becoming the first black woman member of the cabinet. Ann Taylor, Margaret Beckett and Jacqui Smith became the first women to hold the offices of Chief Whip, Foreign Secretary and Home Secretary respectively. And more women have served in cabinets since 1997 than during the whole of the preceding 80 years. All this has impacted on policy-making at the highest levels, and continues to do so.

There also is evidence in the devolved institutions in Scotland and Wales that the relatively high number of women (33.3% of the Scottish Parliament and 48% of the Welsh Assembly) has had a discernable impact on shaping their policy agendas. In both bodies, women parliamentarians have also championed issues such as childcare, the social economy and equal pay.

The Government is committed to equal representation of women and men in political life. We want to see more women in key decision making positions. This is crucial if we are to ensure we have policies that deliver for women, and crucial if Parliament isn't to be seen as irrelevant and dull by the public it serves.

We've already done a lot to address under-representation in political life. For example, we introduced the Sex Discrimination (Election Candidates) Act 2002, enabling political parties to take special measures to boost the number of women standing, local, national and European elections is aimed at all women including BAME and disabled women.

The Equality Bill will extend the time available to political parties to use these special measures to 2030. These provisions are a significant tool in increasing diversity in all aspects of political life from MPs through to local councillors. The Bill will also include a broad range of positive action provisions that will allow political parties and public bodies to take a range of steps to encourage involvement amongst under-represented groups.

The House of Commons has established a Speaker's Conference which is considering the under representation of women, ethnic minorities and disabled people in the House of Commons. This is an important platform to discuss the further action that is needed to make the House more representative of the people it serves. Indeed, to return to the early years of the 20th century once more, the 1916-17 Speaker's Conference achieved a significant milestone for women in securing cross-party agreement on the principle that women should have the right to vote. The Conference led to the Representation of the People Act 1918, which extended the right to vote to women over 30 years old.

However, we still need to go further. Women currently comprise 51% of the population, and 11.32% of the population is Black, Asian or Minority Ethnic (BAME). This means that for Parliament to be truly representative of the country it serves there would need to be 330 female MPs and 316 male MPs, and 32 female BAME MPs. However, there are currently 125 female MPs and 15 ethnic minority MPs, only two of whom are women. We still have a long way to go.

At a local level, there is also more to be done. There are around 149 female councillors from ethnic minority backgrounds in England which represents less than 1% of all councillors. To address this under-representation, this would need to be closer to 1000.

We have taken steps to provide practical ways to increase the numbers of BAME women councillors. In May 2008 we launched a cross-party taskforce to raise awareness of the issue and to support women to develop the confidence and skills to step forward in the future. The taskforce is currently running a national outreach campaign and will soon be launching the country's first national BAME Women Councillor Shadowing Scheme, equipping and motivating participants to engage in party politics.

The Government is also taking action to address under-representation in other spheres of public life such as public appointments, building skills and knowledge to enable people from a range of backgrounds to feel more confident in their ability to participate more fully in public life, and encouraging effective role models and networks to support women in positions of leadership.

However, while Government action has increased the number of women in Parliament, Black, Asian and Minority Ethnic (BAME) women remain some of the most under-represented in both public and political life. That is why Government made this one of their priorities for women in July 2007.

Last year saw the marking of such significant anniversaries both in terms of women's right to vote but also in standing in Parliament. We've come a long way since winning the right in vote back in February 1918 and on the same terms as men in 1928.

Labour in government has made a real and tangible difference to women's lives, and it has been able to do this because of the significant number of women MPs it now has. The use of positive action has levelled the playing field for many women in selection procedures, and constructive use of Labour's enabling legislation will ensure that the Party continues to send ever greater numbers of women to parliament.

# A Great Act of Justice

The task of tackling under-representation of women in politics is not necessarily an easy one, but it is a vital one if we are to create the fairer society we all want to see. There is definitely no shortage of talented women who, given half the chance, would make excellent councillors, MEPs and parliamentarians. We must continue to work to ensure that all in our society share the same freedoms and opportunities, so that we can lead the way for future generations.

# Women Liberal Democrats

By and large, the Liberal Party was lukewarm in its advocacy of the enfranchisement of women, although individual Liberals were staunchly supportive and many Liberal women were heavily involved in the suffrage campaign.

One of the reasons for the Liberal Party's ambivalent attitude was that it considered reform of the voting system (i.e., the introduction of proportional representation [PR]) to be more important than any other change, including the enfranchisement of women, and right up to 1928 Liberals wanted to see PR included in any electoral legislation.

Both the Women's Liberal Federation (WLF) and the Liberal Women's Suffrage Society were established in 1887, and Liberal women continued to apply pressure to the party's leadership. By the years before the war, the WLF had more than 150,000 members, and there was every reason to suppose that, once women had the vote, Liberal women would enter parliament at the same rate as those for the other parties.

Unfortunately, the enfranchisement of women coincided with the start of the Liberal Party's electoral decline, and as a result, although a number of prominent Liberal women stood as candidates, they found it very difficult to get elected.

The first Liberal woman to succeed was Margaret Wintringham, who was elected in a by-election in 1921, but lost her seat in 1924. Lady Terrington was elected at the 1923 general election, but also lost again the following year. Hilda Runciman, the third Liberal woman MP, won St Ives in a by-election in 1928, but moved to a more marginal seat for the 1929 general election, leaving her safe seat to her husband.

As a result, only Megan Lloyd George represented the Liberal Party in the 1929 intake of women MPs, and she remained the only Liberal woman MP until 1951, when she was defeated. She then defected to the Labour Party, so that when she returned to parliament in a by-election in 1957 she did so as a Labour member.

Between 1951 and 1987, when Ray Michie was elected, the Liberal Party had no women MPs at all. The Social Democratic Party (SDP), which was set up in 1981, had one woman MP in the shape of Shirley Williams, but she lost her seat before it merged with the Liberal Party.

In 1992 Ray Michie was joined by Liz Lynne, and then by Diana Maddock and Emma Nicholson, both of whom were elected in by-elections. Three Liberal Democrat women were elected in 1997, five in 2001, and ten in 2005.

The sudden increase in the number of women being elected was due at least in part to the establishment in 2001 of the Campaign for Gender Balance, the principal objective of which was to get more Liberal Democrat women elected. This group's current target is that 40% of new Liberal Democrat MPs should be women after the next election. Candidate selections made to date suggest that this may be achievable, and that, in terms of the percentage of women MPs, the party's progress should continue.

This has been achieved without the use of the positive action mechanisms adopted by Labour, which the Liberal Democrat Party as a whole and many Liberal Democrat women individually opposed. The relatively small number of Liberal Democrat seats available may have made this easier, and, whatever happens at the next election the actual number of Liberal Democrat women will probably remain low; however, the strategies the party has used have clearly worked, and suggest that, in some circumstances, effective alternatives to AWS are available.

There are currently four women in the Liberal Democrat shadow cabinet, although only two of them are in what would normally be considered cabinet roles, the others falling into the 'also attends cabinet' category.

It is a pity that the contribution of Liberal women to the suffrage campaign should have been obscured by their party's subsequent decline, and the complete absence of women from the Liberal benches for over thirty years did not reflect the strength that women in the party had previously had. The complete absence of women from the Liberal benches for over thirty years would have appalled them; this absence is now being addressed with some success and this trend looks as though it will continue.

# Celebrating Progress: Encouraging More
## by Jo Swinson MP

*Former marketing manager Jo Swinson was elected MP for East Dunbartonshire in May 2005. She is Lib Dem Shadow Minister for Foreign Affairs, and serves on the Environmental Audit Select Committee.*

*Jo chaired the Lib Dem Campaign for Gender Balance (www.genderbalance.org.uk) from 2006 – 2008, and is a member of the Speaker's Conference looking at ways to increase the number of women and BME MPs (www.parliament.uk/speakersconference).*

*Until recently, Jo was the youngest MP.*

**Let me take you on a tour of Parliament**

A couple of months after I was elected, I went on the official tour of the Houses of Parliament, as I figured I really ought to know a bit more about the institution I had been elected to serve in. Being shown around the building by an expert tour guide with a vast knowledge of Parliament's history and heritage was absolutely fascinating; in fact I would recommend the tour to anyone (and it can be booked for free through your local MP).

Wonderful as it was to see the finery of the House of Lords, the grandeur of the chilly and cavernous Westminster Hall, and the macabre interest of looking at the death warrant of Charles I, none of these were my favourite part of the tour.

The best bit, in my opinion, is hearing the tale of one fairly unremarkable marble statue in St Stephen's Hall, that of the second Viscount Falkland. The tour guide draws attention to a hairline fracture in the sword that Falkland is plunging into the marble plinth at his feet.

This is where on 27th April 1909 one brave suffragette, Miss Margery Humes, chained herself to the statue to protest to MPs about votes for women. In order to remove her, the sword had to be broken, and the repair is still visible today. It took another decade for women to win the right to vote, and it wasn't until twenty years later, in 1929, that women could vote on the same terms as men.

Since then we've had twenty General Elections, and women now make up 20% of our MPs. In some ways, I think this is fantastic progress. When my 96-year old grandmother was born, women could not vote. Within her lifetime she has seen women win the vote, win elections, and hold key offices of state including Prime Minister.

At the same time, the pace of change can feel frustratingly slow. Parliament often seems stuck in a time warp – in more ways than one – and especially when you look at the gender representation. It affects the culture and the atmosphere: aggressive, confrontational, petty point-scoring. I'm not saying that no women MPs engage in this kind of behaviour in the House of Commons, but the puerile nature of some debates and question sessions is worryingly reminiscent of unruly boys in a boarding school. The etymology is revealing: puer is the Latin word for boy.

**A wonderfully rewarding job**

That said, the job of an MP is a fabulous one. Being able to devote your life to the causes you feel passionately about, and stand up for people in the area you live is a great motivation for getting out of bed in the morning!

Contrary to popular belief, being an MP is not all about making speeches. There's an element of public speaking, but mostly to small groups in the constituency, and it gets much easier (and less stressful!) with practice. Most of my time is actually spent listening to the views of local people and trying to work out solutions to problems in the constituency, and then taking up those issues in Parliament.

Even Parliament is much more consensual and constructive than is portayed by the media. Sitting on a Select Committee means working across party lines, hearing evidence from experts and making recommendations to Government. PMQs aside, many sessions in the House of Commons chamber allow genuine, interesting debate instead of political theatre.

The skills of negotiating, empathising with people, and bringing people together are ones that come naturally to many women. While the timings of key events like votes or Committee debates are determined by others, as an MP you are essentially your own boss, which means much of your diary can be organised around your life and commitments. You can plan your Parliamentary and constituency appointments such that you guarantee time for the non-work stuff, whether it's visiting your 95-year old grandmother or attending your child's school parents' evening.

Those involved in politics need to do better at "selling" the job of an MP, if we are to attract under-represented groups who currently think it isn't for them. I very much hope that one of the outcomes of the Speaker's Conference will be for Parliament to undertake specific outreach work to encourage people to consider standing for election.

Most women MPs I speak to would not have stood were it not for someone else suggesting the idea. I know that is certainly the case for me. Let's face it, not many people wake up one morning and think "I want to be an MP".

**Needed: a confidence boost for women**
Another issue which holds back many women and girls is confidence, or lack of it. I often speak to groups of local schoolchildren about the role of an MP and politics in general. It is disappointing when the vast majority of the time, it is the boys in the class who are first to put their hands to go up to ask questions. Sometimes the first eight or ten questions have been from boys and I have had to specifically ask the girls to contribute.

Yet I remember that feeling in class myself, and later in life in a political context, such as fringe meetings at party conference. Thinking of a question or comment in your head, and a little voice undermining you, saying it would sound silly. Weighing up whether or not to be brave and speak up, and in the meantime one of the blokes asks it – in a less eloquent way – and everyone nods in approval.

We need to teach girls from an early age how to make their voices heard, and recognise that the habits of a lifetime may mean that women sometime need an extra encouragement or nudge to get involved.

That's why Michelle Obama was spot on recently when she spoke to 100 London schoolgirls, encouraging them to aim high, and be the best they can be. Afterwards many of them spoke about how powerful that message was. There are millions of women and girls in the UK who need that message, who will flourish with that confidence boost.

At the risk of controversy, I'd say that no doesn't always mean no – at least when a woman is talking about getting involved in politics. I've lost count of the times when I've suggested standing for Parliament to someone, and they've dismissed the idea, only to end up going for it months or years later, after similar overtures from more people. Sometimes the idea needs to be sown in the back of their mind, to niggle away until it finally takes root.

**Performing the juggling act: childcare and politics**
One serious and stubborn barrier to women's full involvement in our political life is the continuing inequality over caring responsibilities, in particular childcare. Being a Parliamentary candidate and having a full-time job is demanding enough – throw children into the mix and you can see why so many women opt-out. In particular, women opt-out just at the point that many of their male counterparts are getting elected.

It is revealing that of the 9 Lib Dem women MPs, all of us either have no children, or have grown-up children. Even the number of Labour women MPs with young children is small. Look at the male MPs, however, and it's a very different story.

Societal gender imbalances in who shoulders the childcare responsibility put women at a huge disadvantage. Changing the way society looks at bringing up children will not happen overnight. However some basic changes could be made to improve the situation, not least creating space for childcare facilities in the House of Commons (yes, we have a shooting gallery, but no crèche!). Sitting until the early hours of the morning is a thing of the past, but the House still sits until 10pm twice a week, with the timing of votes often unpredictable.

If we don't have mothers and fathers of young children able to both play an active part in their children's upbringing and do the job of a Member of Parliament then our democracy will be the poorer for it.

**The next wave of women MPs**

Commemorating the 1929 election brings a good opportunity to assess what has been achieved in terms of women's involvement in politics in the last 80 years. Although we can and should celebrate how far we have come, we must recognise that we're far from the end of the journey to secure equality. Politicians, Parliament, the media and the public all have a role to play in encouraging the next wave of women activists, Councillors and MPs. Pioneering women have shown it can be done, but now we need to make politics a mainstream pursuit for women from all backgrounds. With innovative approaches to combing politics with family, additional effort to promote politics as welcoming to women, and lots of encouragement, I am certain it can be done.

# Women of Other Parties and None

Since 1918, a total of fourteen women not members of either the Conservative, Labour or Liberal (Democrat) parties have entered parliament. Five of them have belonged to the Scottish National Party (SNP), three to the Ulster Unionist Party (UUP), two to Sinn Fein, and one to the Democratic Unionist Party. One was elected on an Independent Unity ticket, one as a genuine Independent, and one – in 2005 – as Speaker of the House, a post which is held on a non-party basis, and the holder of which is therefore traditionally elected unopposed.

Women knew from the beginning that a party affiliation would be necessary, but various attempts were still made to challenge this, or at least to broaden the choice. In 1918 Christabel Pankhurst stood in Smethwick for the Women's Party, but was not successful and the Women's Party, despite later efforts to revive it, soon fell by the wayside.

Women also stood in the early years as independents, but, with the exception of Eleanor Rathbone in 1929, failed to be elected.

The political ideologies and structures between which women thus had to choose had been developed over the preceding century by men, and there is no doubt that in all three parties women found it difficult to fit in. The political culture was – and remains – fiercely combative, and the more collaborative ways of working, which had been developed particularly by the suffrage movement, were not regarded as having value. The parties took different routes to 'integrate' the new women members, but generally these relied upon separate organizations and therefore restricted access to the highest levels.

This has now changed to some extent, and the increase in the number of electable parties in some parts of Britain has offered women other opportunities, although in the current parliament neither the SNP nor Plaid Cymru have women representatives, all three of the women not belonging to the 'big three' being from Northern Ireland. In practice, this means only two, since the Sinn Fein MP has not taken her seat.

It is possible that changes in the political culture in the next few years may increase the number of women standing for smaller parties, or for no party at all; constitutional changes or changes in voting methods may also have an effect. In the meantime, the vast majority of women MPs will continue to be drawn from the three largest parties.

*A Great Act of Justice*

# Women in Europe

The European Parliament has been directly elected since 1979, and although it has seen many changes in terms of the number of countries who send representatives to it, the overall trend in terms of women members has been upwards.

35% of Members of the European Parliament (MEPs) are now women, as opposed to 16% in 1979. In that year only 14% of the UK's MEPs were women; this figure now stands at 33%.

Finland has the highest percentage of women MEPs, with Malta, with none, at the bottom of the league table. The UK is ranked nineteenth out of the twenty-seven member states, with countries such as Sweden (56%), France (44%) and Romania (36%) above it and Ireland (25%), Italy (25%) and Poland (22%) below.[1]

Unlike the Westminster parliament, the European parliament is elected using a system of proportional representation (PR), and this has undoubtedly contributed to the higher numbers of women MEPs across the board. In the UK, the use of a regional list system means that parties are more easily able to secure some form of gender balance than they can for single-member constituencies electing on first-past-the-post systems. However, because the lists are ranked, with those at the top standing a far greater chance of election than those at the bottom, women's chances of success are also dependent upon their being placed in the first three on their party's list.

Thus, although the representation of women as UK MEPs has continued to move in the right direction overall, it remains linked to both the electoral system used and the decisions of individual political parties about candidates. If parties which do well at elections field high numbers of women candidates, and field them in winnable positions on the list, then both the number and the percentage of women being elected will continue to rise.

It is also the case that the UK has, since the inception of the European Parliament, lagged behind the majority of member countries in terms of women's representation, and this has been the case regardless of the size or composition of the European Union. However, the representation of UK women in the European parliament significantly exceeds that at Westminster, and is likely to continue to do so for some time.

---

[1] Figures from the European Parliament website at www.europarl.europaeu/parliament/archive/elections 2009

# A European perspective
# by Linda McAvan MEP

*Linda McAvan is the Labour MEP for the Yorkshire & the Humber region, and is her party's spokesperson in the European Parliament on environment, public health & food safety issues. She serves as vice chair of the Joint African, Caribbean and Pacific-European Union Assembly, and was the only Labour MEP to sit on the Convention on the Future of Europe which was responsible for drafting the EU Constitution. She was first elected to the European Parliament in 1998, and her special interests include fair trade and economic regeneration.*

**How long have** we had equal voting rights for all in Britain? In living memory, over a hundred years, over 200 years? This is a question I often ask students when visiting local schools and colleges. More often than not, they tend to assume that the answer is a very long time and certainly not recent history. That is why I feel it is important that we mark the anniversary of the "Flappers" election in 1929 because it is a useful reminder that full voting rights for all citizens in our country were a long time coming- and that they cannot be taken for granted.

Britain was not, of course, the first country to give votes to women. New Zealand and Finland share that honour, being the first in the world and the first in Europe respectively. But in the past 80 years, the struggle for gender equality has continued across Europe. Much progress has been made, and more women have made their mark on politics. This is especially true at European level, as the European Parliament has one of the highest levels of representation of women in an elected political institution anywhere in the world. It is made up of 785 MEPs, a third of which are women. Whilst this does not constitute an equal gender balance, it still boasts a much better representation of women than many EU Member State governments and other democracies. And women are among the most active MEPs, holding a number of key positions.

Having a high representation of women has, I believe, made its mark on the legislation that has emanated from the European Parliament. European law has created a legal requirement for equal pay for men and women, and has ensured better rights for both part time (often women) and pregnant workers. This legislation is helping to reduce the gender pay gap and making it easier for women to balance work and family life. Within the institution itself, the European Parliament has a Women's Rights and Gender Equality Committee which has been instrumental in pressing for measures to combat human trafficking (which disproportionately affects women) and in promoting gender equality as a fundamental human right. We are also very active on overseas development policy and ensuring that the interests of women are not forgotten across the whole range of policies.

Does the higher percentage of women make for a different style of working than the male dominated parliaments? Certainly, there is less "yah-boo" politics than at Westminster. There is no dominant majority or opposition party in the European Parliament. Every piece of legislation depends on building a coalition of MEPs from different countries and different political groups to support it. Shouting down your opponents is not enough. A good European legislator is one who is a good negotiator, listens to their opponents and builds a consensus. Now these characteristics are not exclusively the preserve of women. And a number of my UK colleagues who were MPs, both men and women, have told me that they prefer our style of working and feel that they can have a bigger say over lawmaking in the European Parliament than a backbench MP back home. But when I recently worked on a very contentious law on climate change with mainly women MEPs from a range of countries and of very different political persuasions, I have to say that I found we worked very efficiently and got speedy results. A senior diplomat – a man – expressed his astonishment at our rapid progress through the thorny issues, telling us that unlike some of our male counterparts, we just got on with it, leaving out egos at the door.

And how representative are women MEPs of the average woman voter? No detailed research has been done on this. One fact that is worth noting is that fewer than 50% of female MEPs have children, which is perhaps indicative of some of the problems that women face if they want a career in politics. Women with young families can find it particularly difficult and the regular, often long-distance travel makes the working life of an MEP particularly unappealing for someone with a young family. But the reality is that many working women, regardless of their job, face similar difficulties in terms of balancing work and family life. This needs to be tackled head-on. And one way to do that is by having more women elected. The election of over a hundred Labour women MPs in the UK in 1997 and the resulting increase in female representation at ministerial level has, in my view, led to issues such as access to childcare and work-life balance becoming priorities for UK government action.

The most recent European Elections took place in June 2009 and marked the 30th anniversary of the directly elected European Parliament, a Parliament whose first ever President (equivalent to a British "Speaker") was a woman, the French holocaust survivor Simone Weil. The new European Parliament has seen an increase in the number of women represented, including from the UK. Many countries now have a system of quotas/zipping on lists to ensure gender parity. A more balanced Parliament should therefore follow.

Writing this article, I realised that my grandmother who died in her mid 90s a few years ago, probably voted for the first time in the Flappers election. A working class woman who left school at fourteen to work in a mill, I doubt she would have recognised herself in the term "Flapper". But I wish now that I had asked her what it felt like to be among that first generation of women who saw the beginning of true equality in Britain's voting laws. They really did make a difference.

*A Great Act of Justice*

# UK Women Members of the European Parliament

Members in the list below were all elected in June 2009, and constitute 35% of UK MEPs. MEPs represent regions/nations of the UK rather than individual constituencies.

|  | **Region** | **Party** |
|---|---|---|
| Marta Andreason | South East | UKIP |
| Catherine Bearder | South East | Liberal Democrat |
| Sharon Bowles | South East | Liberal Democrat |
| Bairbre de Brun | Northern Ireland | Sinn Fein |
| Diane Dodds | Northern Ireland | Democratic Unionist |
| Jill Evans | Wales | Plaid Cymru |
| Vicky Ford | Eastern | Conservative |
| Jacqueline Foster | North West | Conservative |
| Julie Girling | South West | Conservative |
| Fiona Hall | North East | Liberal Democrat |
| Mary Honeyball | London | Labour |
| Jean Lambert | London | Green |
| Caroline Lucas | South East | Green |
| Baroness Sarah Ludford | London | Liberal Democrat |
| Elizabeth Lynne | West Midlands | Liberal Democrat |
| Linda McAvan | Yorkshire & Humber | Labour |
| Arlene McCarthy | North West | Labour |
| Emma McClarkin | East Midlands | Conservative |
| Nicole Sinclaire | West Midlands | UKIP |
| Catherine Stihler | Scotland | Labour |
| Kay Swinburne | Wales | Conservative |
| Diana Wallis | Yorkshire & Humber | Liberal Democrat |
| Glennis Wilmott | East Midlands | Labour |
| Marina Yannakoudakis | London | Conservative |

# Women in Devolved Institutions

The last decade has seen the development of a new aspect of British politics – devolved governmental institutions in Scotland, Wales and Northern Ireland.

Both the names and the scope of these bodies vary; Scotland has a parliament, and Wales and Northern Ireland have assemblies, which have fewer powers. All three are led by First Ministers, and all three First Ministers are men.

However, the newness of these institutions has allowed some parties to be more flexible in their candidate selection policies, and this, combined with the fact that all three use proportional representation has meant that the level of women elected to them has been significantly higher than for the Westminster parliament.

34% of members of the Scottish parliament (MSPs) are women, and 47% of members of the Welsh Assembly (ASPs). The Welsh Assembly was, in its initial set of elections, the first legislative body in the world in which more than 50% of its members were women, but this fell back in subsequent elections.

In Northern Ireland, which has arrived at devolution through a very different route, the percentage of women members of the legislative assembly (MLAs) is, at 17%, very low, and is likely to take some time to increase.

There are several other elected legislatures in the islands of the Irish Sea and the Channel.

The Isle of Man's Tynwald claims to be the oldest parliament in the world, and its directly elected chamber, the House of Keys, has 25 members. Of these, only two (8%) are women.

Eight out of fifty (16%) of members of the States of Guernsey are women. In the Bailiwick of Jersey there are three groups of elected members of the States Assembly – Senators (one woman out of twelve), Connetables (two women out of twelve), and Deputies (nine women out of twenty-nine) – in total, women constitute 24% of elected members. Nine (32%) of the island of Sark's recently elected Conseillers are women, and one of the ten members of the States of Alderney.

The three contributions which follow look at the position in Wales, Scotland and Northern Ireland since devolution.

A Great Act of Justice

# Women in Politics in Wales
# by Baroness Anita Gale

*Anita Gale is the former General Secretary of the Wales Labour Party. She retired in 1999 when she was appointed a Life Peer. She was the Equalities Officer for the Labour Organisers Branch of the GMB 1990-1999.*

*She serves on the Board of the Women's National Commission as the Commissioner for Wales. he is a member of the UK delegation to the Parliamentary Assembly of the Council of Europe, and serves on the Equal Opportunities for women and men committee.*

*Anita chairs the All Party Parliamentary Group on Parkinson's disease, and is a Patron of Kidney Wales Foundation.*

*Her main interests include women and equalities, Welsh affairs and children's rights.*

*She has always been interested in the progress of women in the political life of Wales, and is fascinated in reading the history of women's involvement, and of their struggles to achieve recognition.*

**During my political life** I have seen some improvements, but all too slow and long battles fought to achieve any advancement.

It has been a long hard journey since 1929 when the first woman was elected as a member of parliament for a Welsh constituency. Lady Megan Lloyd George the daughter of David Lloyd George became the Liberal MP for Anglesey. It took until the 1950 general election before two other women joined her. Eirene White was elected MP for East Flintshire and Dorothy Rees for Barry.

At the 1951 general election Dorothy Rees and Lady Megan had lost their seats. Eirene White was the only women MP elected.

The Carmarthen by-election of 1957 saw Lady Megan making a comeback when she stood as the Labour candidate taking the seat from the Liberals holding the seat until her death in 1966. This by election was notable for being the first election in the United Kingdom in which two women competed for the same seat, as Plaid Cymru fielded a woman candidate.

# The Flapper Election and After

Eirene White retired at the 1970 general election. There were no women MPs in Wales for the next 14 years.

When Ann Clwyd was elected for Cynon Valley at a by election in 1984 she was the first woman to be elected to a safe Labour seat in Wales. She was the only woman MP until 1997 when three Labour women who were selected using all women short lists. Betty Williams was elected for Conwy, a seat previously held by the Conservatives, Jackie Lawrence was elected for Preseli Pembrokeshire, a new seat created because of boundary changes, and Julie Morgan was elected for Cardiff North taking the seat from the Conservatives.

The four were re-elected in the general election in 2001. The interesting fact about this election was that ten male MP's retired. Of the ten male MPs who stood down, ten male candidates were selected in their place and all were elected. What a lost opportunity for getting more women MP's! The law of averages should have allowed some women to have been selected, but it seems these laws do not apply to Wales.

Doesn't this highlight the problems for women in Wales? It seems to me that all doors are closed to potential women politicians in Wales without special measures, like all women short lists.

But let's look at the 2005 general election. What happened there?

Good things I am glad to say. Labour once again used all women shortlists in the three Labour seats of Llanelli, Swansea East, and Newport East where the male MPs retired.

Madeline Moon was selected as the candidate for Bridgend, only the second women ever to be selected for a Labour held seat on an open list. Following the general election there were eight women MPs in Wales, the largest number ever. Seven Labour and one Liberal Democrat.

Looking at how difficult it is for women to become MPs in Wales, how is that there are so many women in the Welsh Assembly?

At the first elections in 1999, being a brand new institution gave political parties their one and only opportunity to try something new. Three out of the four parties did use some form of positive measures.

I believe it was essential that at the first elections in 1999 there should be a good number of women elected. As Labour would probably win most of its seats in the Constituency section, where there would be 40 seats it was essential that Labour fielded 20 women candidates and that they would fight winnable seats. And as far as I was concerned it was not only about getting Labour women candidates, it was also about presenting a new image of Wales reflecting the devolved Wales. A new start, a new beginning.

The Labour Party's plan was 'twinning' or 'pairing'. This was a system where women and men would have an equal chance in the selection procedure. Implementing this policy took a lot of courage. There was much debate, and disagreement amongst party members. It was a long hard battle where all the prejudices against women came to the fore. It was difficult, but it was achieved and Labour fielded an equal number of men and women candidates.

At the first general election to the Welsh Assembly in May 1999 Wales was transformed. Women made up 40% of the elected members from the Labour Party, Plaid Cymru and the Liberal Democrats. Only the Conservatives had no women elected. Not only did we have a devolved government but never before had there been so many women politicians. Women who would serve as such positive role models for the new Wales. Women who would make the difference.

At the Welsh Assembly general election of 2003, 30 women and 30 men were elected, the first and only democratic institution in the world to have an equal number of women and men. Owing to a by election in 2006 when a women was elected it took the number of women to 31.

Has having a large number of women in the Welsh Assembly changed much in Wales for women?

Women politicians have certainly had a high profile with women in the Cabinet holding important portfolios such as education, health, and finance. They are visible, and provide good role models. Much has been written about the women in the Welsh Assembly. It is a unique institution being the first in the world to have an equal number of women and men.

In contrast to the great success of women in the Welsh Assembly a report published recently by the Equalities and Human Rights Commission Wales "*Who runs Wales 2009*" makes depressing reading, showing that in all walks of life women in Wales still have a long road to travel to achieve equality. At all levels, be it business, media, industry, or public bodies men are in charge, and women are far behind. This is a serious matter. Wales is losing out on so much because women are unable to use their talents to the full.

I consider that the lack of equality and diversity in most institutions in Wales requires drastic action. How can Wales be changed? What can be done?

I believe action should be taken to resolve the problem of the under representation of women in the life of Wales.

We know what works. All women shortlists work. Pairing or twinning works. Quota systems work. Zipping works for the selection of women candidates where the method of election is by a list or proportional representation.

What I propose is the establishment of a Convention which would examine the under representation of women in political and public life. It would look at why so few women are able to achieve their full potential, and what barriers prevent them playing their full part. The Convention would come forward with solutions, or measures which when implemented would guarantee women being allowed to play a full role in all walks of life. All major institutions in Wales – such as the CBI Wales, the Wales TUC, the Welsh Local Government Association, NGOs in Wales, the four main political parties, the churches, Welsh Women's Aid and community groups – would be invited to take part, working together to discuss what actions could be taken to improve the opportunities for women. The Convention could be facilitated by the Equality and Human Rights Commission in Wales.

This could be a pilot scheme that the rest of the UK could follow. I trust that this idea is taken seriously so that women would no longer be in a position where they are unable to play their full part in the political and public life of Wales.

The women of Wales deserve to be treated equally. They have proved that in the Welsh Assembly women are capably of hold tough portfolios proving that women politicians can get things done, and make a difference.

What better way of mark this 90th anniversary than to agree that women in Wales have been under represented for far too long, and that action needs to be taken to change this situation.

By accepting this there will be recognition that no longer will we allow the talents of women to go unrecognised. Then we will be truly able to say that Wales, and women will flourish together. What a wonderful way to prepare for the advancement of women in the next 90 years.

# 'Quietly thrilling': Women and the Scottish Parliament by Fiona Mackay

*Fiona Mackay is Senior Lecturer in Politics at the University of Edinburgh. Current research focuses on gender and constitutional change in the UK. She is co-author of Women, politics and constitutional change (University of Wales Press 2007), author of Love and Politics (Continuum 2001), and co-editor of The Changing Politics of Gender Equality in Britain (Palgrave 2002) and Women and Contemporary Scottish Politics (Polygon 2001). She was active in the 50/50 campaign for gender parity in political and public life in the run up to devolution.*

## Introduction

'Actually to see a parliament with so many women is quietly thrilling, in a way that percentages are not [...] I expected the Scottish Parliament to look different, but it doesn't. It looks like the rest of life, where women and men are present in roughly equal numbers except when gender segregation is imposed – openly or otherwise – for a special reason. (Sue Innes, feminist journalist, campaigner and writer 2001: 249)

The quiet thrill – expressed by the late Sue Innes, was shared by many Scottish women – trade unionists, feminists, community and party activists, and devolution campaigners – who were part of the broad coalition campaigning for equal political power in the new Scottish parliament. Opportunities for 'women-friendly' change are created by reform processes, and the chance to be in at the start of a new institution. The most notable and visible achievement has been the high level of women's political representation: the first parliament returned 37.2 per cent female MSPs, far outstripping Westminster. This was as a result of the adoption of one-off quota-type mechanisms by Scottish Labour, which were matched by informal – but effective – intervention by their biggest political rival, the Scottish National Party (SNP). The proportion of women rose again to 39.5 per cent in the second elections in 2003, seemingly heralding a new gender settlement in Scottish politics.

The institutional 'blueprints' of the parliament also contained important statements and mechanisms for promoting gender equality and equal opportunities. Key features included: 'family friendly' working hours for the parliament and the recognition of Scottish school holidays; a purpose-built visitors' crèche; a Parliamentary Equal Opportunities Committee with a remit for equal opportunities issues both inside and outside the parliament; an Equality Unit within the Scottish government, tasked with promoting multiple strands of equality; the commitment of both parliament and government to 'mainstream' equality – including gender equality – across all their areas of work including legislation and policy-making. The key principles adopted by both parliament and government promote more open, accessible decision-making processes and more participatory politics.

However, experience points to the importance of what follows after a period of reform; there is no automatic or guaranteed translation from principles to practice. In this short paper, I will discuss briefly what has happened in the intervening decade. My own research concentrated, primarily, on the first Scottish parliament (1999-2003) therefore some of my comments necessarily are impressionistic.

It will come as no surprise that the reality is messy and complex, changes are circumscribed and gains have been contingent. The designers of the Scottish Parliament, including women, had aspirations to create a new institution that would depart from the standard Westminster model and promote a different political culture. However alongside change are many elements of institutional and cultural continuity such as tendencies towards political centralisation, strong party discipline and executive dominance. Early (almost certainly unrealistic) aspirations and expectations have been disappointed.

Apart from demonstrating 'fair play' or justice, the presence of women in substantial numbers in political institutions brings with it a set of expectations: that women will 'improve' the style and conduct of politics and, more controversially, that women politicians will 'act for' women and on their behalf, leading to substantive policy outcomes. Studies of the first years of the Scottish parliament provide some evidence to support each of these contentions but the overall message delivered is that the politics of presence in practice is complex. The relationship between 'being there' and substantive outcomes is by no means straightforward and is mediated by other factors, most particularly in strong party parliamentary systems by party identity and partisan loyalties.

## Civilising politics? Feminising politics?

A consensus is apparent amongst commentators and politicians that the culture of the Scottish parliament is more civilised and more civil than that of Westminster. I have argued that this is as a consequence, in combination, of new rules and structures, the alternative norms provided by 'new politics', and the substantial female presence. As one woman MSP remarked, *'I think some of the men have learned that to get things done you have to act in a different way.'* Whilst simple assumptions that numbers alone provide adequate explanations of political change have been discredited, nevertheless proportions appear to play some role. For example, The Scottish parliament with a 60/40 balance and with some apparent 'regendering' of political norms has a culture of civility and mutual respect and has largely avoided the 'yah boo' adversarial practices of Westminster. The public expression of sexualised language or sexist attitudes is rare and regarded as unparliamentary. Challenges to institutional innovations such as the statutory Equal Opportunities and Public Petitions Committees, the visitors crèche, and the 'family-friendly' sitting hours of the parliament have to date been successfully resisted.

By contrast, Westminster with its 80/20 split and its embedded traditions, routinely doles out 'sexist insults, hostility and boorish behaviour despite the influx of female MPs' to the House of Commons.[2] MSPs have lined up to testify to the more women-friendly culture of the Scottish Parliament and even the somewhat unreconstructed Scottish media have asserted: 'it's a different story at the Scottish Parliament.'[3] These testimonials suggest significant differences in the gendered political culture of the two institutions and in the perceived legitimacy of women and their exercise of authority and leadership. In contrast to Westminster, where women still can be perceived as outsiders, in the Scottish parliament, women politicians feel a sense of entitlement; in turn, their presence is regarded as normal and unremarkable.

## Representing women: policy outcomes

Action against domestic violence has been the most obvious concrete gain for a classic women's agenda. Tackling domestic violence has a stated high priority of public policy in Scotland with cross party support. The agenda has been driven forward as a result of sustained campaigning by women's organisations, particularly the women's refuge movement, and strong political leadership provided by women ministers and female parliamentarians, together with some key male allies. The urgency with which DV was tackled in Scotland in comparison with Westminster is indicative of potential difference that substantial proportions of women politicians in a new institution has made. Scotland tackled the issue in a strategic way early and first: it produced the first national strategy, the first national prevention strategy and the first national training strategy in the UK. Scotland also pioneered improvements in data collection and service development, ring-fenced funding, and the national domestic abuse telephone helpline. A recent UK-wide survey of specialist violence against women support services found that service provision in Scotland was distributed more equally than elsewhere. *The Maps of Gaps* report, jointly commissioned by the End Violence Against Women and the Equality and Human Rights Commission commended the strategic, gendered and integrated approach in Scotland as 'benchmark' against which developments elsewhere in the UK should be measured (Coy et al, 2007).

## Conclusions

Overall, despite shortfalls, slippages and sets backs there is a relatively positive story to tell. There have been discernible impacts that relate not only to the presence and actions of women politicians – particularly feminist and equality champions – and their male allies, but also to the more general 'new politics' ethos of the parliament. However, there are concerns also about faltering commitment and competing priorities. The results of the 2007 Scottish Parliament elections were historic, with the SNP ending over fifty years of Labour dominance of Scottish politics. Yet, the elections also provided a cautionary tale, with the first drop in the number of elected female MSPs since the creation of the parliament in 1999. The proportion fell from 39.5 per cent in 2003 to 33.3 per cent (although it has subsequently risen to 34.8 per cent). Overall, trends in the recruitment and selection of female candidates are also in decline (Mackay and Kenny 2007). This suggests that there is no room for complacency as the parliament enters its second decade.

## References

Coy, M., Kelly, L. and Foord, J. (2007) *Map of Gaps: The Postcode Lottery of Violence Against Women Support Services*. London: End Violence Against Women and Equality and Human Rights Commission. www.endviolenceagainstwomen.org.uk Last accessed November 29, 2008

Innes, S. (2001) '"Quietly thrilling": Women in the New Parliament.' In E. Breitenbach and F. Mackay (eds) Women and Contemporary Scottish Politics: An Anthology. pp.249-253

Mackay, F. and M. Kenny (2007) 'Women's Representation in the 2007 Scottish Parliament: Temporary Setback or Return to the Norm?', Scottish Affairs, 60, pp. 25-38.

---

[2] Jackie Ashley 'Bullied, patronised and abused- women MPs reveal the truth about life inside Westminster' *The Guardian*, December 7, 2004.
[3] Rachel Williams 'Sexist attitudes still a problem in the Commons' *Evening News* December 7, 2004

# Women in Politics in Northern Ireland
## by Bronagh Hinds

*Bronagh Hinds is a consultant and, as director of DemocraShe, established in 2000 to empower women in the political and policy process, is involved in the Women in Local Councils initiative. She was a Senior Fellow at Queen's University Institute of Governance for six years, Deputy Chief Commissioner of the Equality Commission from 1999-2003 and took part in the 1996-98 multi party talks leading to the Belfast (Good Friday) Agreement on behalf of the Women's Coalition. She spent over twenty years in the voluntary sector serving as director of Gingerbread and the Ulster People's College with a period as regional director of Oxfam in between. She was an active member of the Northern Ireland Women's Rights Movement in the 1970s and the founder and first chair of the Northern Ireland Women's European Platform. She is currently the Northern Ireland Commissioner on the UK Women's National Commission and a Commissioner on the Northern Ireland Local Government Staff Commission. She was selected UK Woman of Europe in 1999 and received the International Women's Democracy Center's Global Democracy Award in 2002.*

**In 1996 the male dominance** of politics was shaken – just a little – by the emergence of the Northern Ireland Women's Coalition. An election was held that year for the Northern Ireland Forum for Political Dialogue[4]; it was the entry point to the multi-party talks that led to the Good Friday Agreement in 1998. The Women's Coalition secured just over 1% of the vote, but it was sufficient to get them elected in ninth place as one of the top ten parties.[5]

---

[4] Fifteen women were elected to the Northern Ireland Forum for Political Dialogue. However, the negotiation of the Good Friday Agreement involved the leadership of parties who did not include their women members.

[5] The top ten parties were: Ulster Unionist Party, Social Democratic and Labour Party, Democratic Unionist Party, Sinn Fein, Alliance Party, United Kingdom Unionist Party, Progressive Unionist Party, Democratic Unionist Party, Northern Ireland Women's Coalition and Labour Coalition.

It was a remarkable achievement in an election with twenty-four parties on the ballot paper. Formed just seven weeks before the election the Coalition outpolled some long standing parties. The eight parties elected before it were parties with a track record in winning elections or linked to well-known paramilitary organisations. The Women's Coalition was a brand new entity and brand.

What drove women who had never joined a party before to band together to contest this particular election and become a catalyst for gender change, albeit slow, in other parties? The motivation was anger at women's invisibility in politics coupled with the belief that women at the negotiating table would increase the chance of reaching a political accommodation.

The election method adopted in 1996 offered the ideal opportunity.[6] Intended to 'legitimise' paramilitary-linked parties and bring some with a small democratic mandate into talks, women used it to break through the male domination. They intended to inject something radically different; leaders who could bring a different political style to create the climate for a solution; one in which demonisation and prevarication to accomplish obstruction would be replaced with exposing bad behaviour and modelling cooperation to allow problem-solving to flourish.

The Women's Coalition exposed the myth that women in Northern Ireland were not interested in politics. While all candidates were realistic that only the two regional seats could be won, seventy women contested the election giving the Coalition the fifth largest slate. It was an enthusiastic, exciting roller coaster of a ride for novice campaigners that taught many that politics is not rocket science.

Among the Coalition's many contribution to the text of the Belfast (Good Friday) Agreement were specific references to 'the full and equal political participation of women' and 'the advancement of women in public life'. This led to a new post-Agreement initiative, DemocraShe established in 2000, to encourage greater participation of women in all political parties.

Working from election to election DemocraShe's non-partisan education and training platform offered a comprehensive programme to equip, mentor and promote women with the skills and political acumen to run an election campaign; it worked with women candidates and members of their campaign teams. A great many of the 242 women supported over the five years to 2005 achieved success; 50% of the successful of female MLAs in the Northern Ireland Assembly in 2003 and 41% of female councillors in 2005 were DemocraShe alumni.

---

[6] Eighteen constituencies with five seats each, topped up by two seats for each of the top ten parties on votes aggregated across the constituencies.

Yet, the proportion of women politicians at Westminster, Assembly and in local government remains low in Northern Ireland in 2009: 16.6% in Westminster and the Assembly[7] and 22% in local government. Nationalist women fare better than unionist women with a nod by their parties towards changing the imbalance; but no party has adopted a strategic and targeted plan to deliver consistent results. Resistance persists to making use of the positive action that has been legally permitted since 2002.

Women are better represented in government, although the stability of the government was itself under threat for a good part of the decade following the 1998 Agreement.[8] The first Northern Ireland Executive began with two and ended with three women – Brid Rodgers of the Social Democratic and Labour Party, Bairbre de Brún of Sinn Fein and Carmel Hanna of the SDLP. Leaving aside the joint post of First and Deputy First Minister women hold 4 out of 10 senior ministerial positions in 2009[9] – Arlene Foster of the Democratic Unionist Party, Michelle Gildernew and Caitriona Ruane of Sinn Fein and Margaret Ritchie of the SDLP.

Politics in Northern Ireland has never been easy, its excessively male culture exacerbated by the aggressive and brutal language and extreme tension and rivalry inherent in violent conflict. The Women's Coalition challenged bullying behaviour, sought in vain to have gender-neutral terms used and proposed the adoption of a code of practice on sexual harassment which was regarded as an unwarranted constraint on the behaviour of members of the Forum for Political Dialogue.

The Coalition's efforts to change the culture by naming unacceptable behaviour and producing carefully researched speeches instead of the customary popular top-of-the-head rhetoric did portray a different image of how a politician should perform. However, throughout the first Assembly it was difficult for women in any party to mainstream gender in the polarised political arena in Northern Ireland when tensions around the constitutional question, power-sharing in government

---

[7] The 14 women elected in 1998 comprised 13% of the first Assembly in 1998: 1 DUP, 2 UUP, 3 SDLP (later 4 on John Hume's resignation), 5 Sinn Fein, 1 Alliance and 2 Women's Coalition. There were 18 elected in 2003: 2 DUP, 2 UUP, 5 SDLP, 7 Sinn Fein and 2 Alliance. The 18 elected in 2007 were: 3 DUP, 0 UUP, 4 SDLP, 8 Sinn Fein, 2 Alliance and 1 PUP.

[8] The first Northern Ireland Executive took up office in December 1999 and ended in suspension in October 2002, with periods where devolution was revoked due to disputes over weapons decommissioning and sectarianism. Ongoing disputes and Stormontgate – controversy about an alleged spy-ring and arrest of the Sinn Fein chief administrator at Stormont. – ensured that government did not function for five years. The second Assembly elected in 2003, in which the DUP and Sinn Fein replaced the UUP and the SDLP as the two largest parties of the four entitled to places in government, remained suspended for its entire term; no ministers were appointed to the Executive. The Executive took up its mantle again on election of the third Assembly in 2007.[8]

[9] There are also two Junior Ministers in the Office of the First and deputy First Minister; both are and have been held by men since the first Assembly in 1998.

and 'wicked' issues like decommissioning, policing and criminal justice were very much alive. The increase in the number of women in the 2003 election made little difference – the second Assembly, well and truly mired in controversy, never met. Worth noting though was that of the eighteen women elected, twelve were nationalist and just four were unionist; [10] Sinn Fein required their constituency groups to rerun selection processes to include at least one woman on candidate lists.

With the Assembly stalled there were two initiatives in 2006. Secretary of State Peter Hain brought women MLAs and councillors together to share knowledge and experience and network; speakers from all parties agreed that political culture was a significant obstacle. DUP MLA, later Minister, Arlene Foster put women's reluctance in coming forward down to Northern Ireland's small 'c' conservatism and violent history combined with the aggressive and adversarial behaviour of male politicians.

Women in Local Councils[11] launched earlier the same year to increase women's leadership among councillors and council officers provided a focal point through which local government and other partners could combine expertise and influence.

Political parties, councils and local government organisations are supported to adopt principles, develop gender action plans and take special initiatives. The project addresses culture change as well as gender-balanced representation and develops partnership between female councillors and staff.

Women in Local Councils can lay claim to some exciting developments and achievements. Every council adopted a Declaration of Principles. Most councils and local government bodies appointed Gender Champions; political and officer champions benefit from regular capacity building workshops, peer support and networking. More than 50% of councils have tailored Gender Action Plans in place and a common monitoring and reporting framework has been piloted. Various councils have instituted 'Visible Women' conferences, women's forums and young women's events to reach women in the community.

Results are emerging: a new Women in Local Councils Award was won by Newtownabbey Council for multi-level work involving councillors, officers and community; Belfast City Council's women councillors and officers joint training programme was adopted as a model of good practice by the IDeA; and Omagh Council won a UK award for its women-only training programme. Northern Ireland is going through extensive local government reorganisation and reform similar to that undertaken elsewhere in the UK; the Women in Local Councils agenda aims to bring about more diverse local government in 2011.

---

[10] The final two belonged to the Alliance Party.
[11] www.womeninlocalcouncils.org.uk

In an Assembly debate in 2007 politicians in all parties declared the need for more women in politics. It was disappointing, however, that a resolution to establish an all-party working group to tackle under-representation of women in politics and calling on the Executive to implement and resource a comprehensive strategy was diluted on a vote of 44 to 43 to noting existing commitment to gender equality stating that 'individuals should obtain positions on merit'. Resistance to positive action is a greater hurdle in Northern Ireland than in other regions of the UK.

# Part Four:

# The Next Level

'We need to pool the complementary knowledge, experience and wisdom of both sexes, and we need also, for the highest places in the State – which require all the wisdom and knowledge that is available – to have a choice of all the adult members of the human race.'

Frederick Pethick-Lawrence MP
speaking in the debate on the second reading of the Bill,
29 March 1928.

# Women Across the World

The United Kingdom in general – and England in particular – tends to think of itself as one of the world leaders in the development of its democracy, but historically this has not always been the case, and in terms of representation Britain can still learn from other countries.

The first country to give women the vote was New Zealand in 1893, although women could not become MPs there until 1919. In 1906, when women in Britain were allowed to become councillors but could not vote in parliamentary elections, Finland elected seventeen women to its parliament.

Once British women had the vote, progress towards any kind of equal representation was painfully slow, and, gradually, the UK has been overtaken by a number of other countries in terms of the gender balance of its legislature.

At the time of writing[12], Rwanda (56% women MPs) leads the way internationally, followed by Sweden (47%) and South Africa (44%). Eight of the top twenty-five nations are in Africa, and nine in Europe.

Switzerland – which, in 1971 was one of the last countries in Europe to enfranchise women – has 28% women MPs, and even Lichtenstein, where women were not able to vote until 1984, has 24% women MPs.

In this context, the UK's 19.5% women in the Westminster parliament looks on the low side, and there is still therefore a lot of work to do before the UK can consider itself a genuine world leader in terms of the breadth of representation in its principal democratic institution.

Other issues have also now entered the debate. Women from BME communities are seriously under-represented, as are disabled women. There are relatively few young women, and only one openly lesbian woman in the House. As a result of the need to consider these and other issues, a Speaker's Conference – led by the Speaker of the House of Commons and made up of MPs – has been set up to look at ways of making parliament more representative and inclusive. This has been taking evidence around the country, and is expected to report before the next general election.

The contributions which follow look at some of these issues from various angles and suggest ways forward.

[12]October 2009

# Women in Parliaments Across the World

The list below shows all those countries whose elected lower houses (i.e., the equivalent of the British House of Commons) contained 25% or more women members as at 30 September 2009. Figures for the UK are at the end. The complete list from which these details are taken[13] gives statistics for 187 countries.

| Ranking | Country | Seats | Women | % Women |
|---|---|---|---|---|
| 1 | Rwanda | 80 | 45 | 56.3% |
| 2 | Sweden | 349 | 164 | 47.0% |
| 3 | South Africa | 400 | 178 | 44.5% |
| 4 | Cuba | 614 | 265 | 43.2% |
| 5 | Iceland | 63 | 27 | 42.9% |
| 6 | Argentina | 257 | 107 | 41.6% |
| 7 | Finland | 200 | 83 | 41.5% |
| 8 | Netherlands | 150 | 62 | 41.3% |
| 9 | Denmark | 179 | 68 | 38.0% |
| 10 | Angola | 220 | 82 | 37.3% |
| 11 | Costa Rica | 57 | 21 | 36.8% |
| 12 | Spain | 350 | 127 | 36.3% |
| 13 | Andorra | 28 | 10 | 35.7% |
| 14 | Belgium | 150 | 53 | 35.3% |
| 15 | Mozambique | 250 | 87 | 34.8% |
| 16 | New Zealand | 122 | 41 | 33.6% |
| 17 | Nepal | 594 | 197 | 33.2% |
| 18 | Germany | 622 | 204 | 32.8% |
| 19 | Ecuador | 124 | 40 | 32.3% |
| 20 | Belarus | 110 | 35 | 31.8% |
| 21 | Uganda | 332 | 102 | 30.7% |
| 22 | Burundi | 118 | 36 | 30.5% |
| 23 | United Republic of Tanzania | 319 | 97 | 30.4% |
| 24 | Guyana | 70 | 21 | 30.0% |

[13] http://www.ipu.org/wmn-e/classif.htm accessed on 8 October 2009

| | | | | |
|---|---|---|---|---|
| 25 | Timor-Leste | 65 | 19 | 29.2% |
| 26 | Switzerland | 200 | 57 | 28.5% |
| 27 | F.Y.R. Macedonia | 120 | 34 | 28.3% |
| 28 | Mexico | 500 | 141 | 28.2% |
| 29 | Austria | 183 | 51 | 27.9% |
| 30 | Afghanistan | 242 | 67 | 27.7% |
| 31 | Peru | 120 | 33 | 27.5% |
| 32 | Namibia | 78 | 21 | 26.9% |
| 33 | Trinidad and Tobago | 41 | 11 | 26.8% |
| 34 | Australia | 150 | 40 | 26.7% |
| 35 | Viet Nam | 493 | 127 | 25.8% |
| 36 | Republic of Moldova | 101 | 26 | 25.7% |
| 37 | Kyrgyzstan | 23 | 90 | 25.6% |
| 38 | Iraq | 275 | 70 | 25.5% |
| " | Suriname | 51 | 13 | 25.5% |
| 39 | Lao People's Democratic Republic | 115 | 29 | 25.2% |
| 40 | Lesotho | 120 | 30 | 25.0% |
| " | Monaco | 24 | 6 | 25.0% |
| 58 | United Kingdom | 646 | 126 | 19.5% |

# Moving Forward by Chris Keates

*Chris Keates is the General Secretary of the NASUWT, the UK's largest teaching union. She graduated in archaeology and history from Leicester University, and taught humanities in two Birmingham comprehensives, before becoming an advisory teacher in the Birmingham LEA Central Support Services. In 1986 she became general secretary of Birmingham, the largest NASUWT branch in the country, and held this role until 1997. She was elected to the union's national executive in 1987. She became the Union's General Secretary in 2004, and since then has led it successfully through a period of expansion. At the time of her appointment she was the only woman to lead one of the ten largest TUC affiliated trade unions.*

**In 1918, Emily Phipps**, the first president of the forerunner of the Union of which I am now the General Secretary, stood for parliament. She was one of the first women to do so, and, although she was defeated, it was a significant event in a life devoted to the suffrage and trade union movements, to feminism, and to the advancement of education, particularly girls' education.

The anniversary of the first election at which men and women voted equally in 1929 is an appropriate occasion upon which to look at our progress since that time.

There can be no doubt that some progress has been made. A raft of equality legislation has been an important catalyst in engendering change. The Sex Discrimination Act has crucial, although the question still lingers about how much it has changed attitudes and culture and how much it has simply driven those inclined to discriminate underground. There are still too many employers who openly and consistently flout the law and do so with impunity.

Although it is over 30 years since the Equal Pay Act, women's pay still lags significantly behind that of men, and today the gender pay gap experienced by full-time women workers stands at 17%. For part-time workers, it is double that at 35%.

The chief underlying causes of the pay gap include the undervaluation of women's work, occupational gender segregation and discrimination in the wider economy.

Add to the mix the diet of stereotyping fed through advertising which produces both overt and subliminal messages that define women's role. If it's technical, it's boys and men. If it's cleaning or caring, it's women. In isolation each may seem innocuous, but the cumulative effect of the constant drip-feed reinforces the message.

Progress made in challenging traditional male-dominated occupational roles, coupled with the growth of women's representation in education and the labour market, and the contribution of education in securing gender equality in the workplace, has led to some interesting reactions.

In teaching, the Government is taking steps to redress the perceived 'imbalance' in the number of women and men teachers and to tackle the perceived dysfunctional effects of a 'feminised' teaching profession.

This new wave of backlash arguments is now locating the problem of boys' educational 'underachievement' with the actions of women teachers and working mothers. Far more angst and handwringing is now being expended on boy's underachievement than was ever the case when the position was reversed. The message should be that the achievement of all young people should be of concern.

There are now generalised claims designed to present men as the newly oppressed and to downplay the real story of the persistent nature of men's economic and political advantage which continues to be the order of the day.

These discourses of male disadvantage are acting to reassert the masculine gender order and reclaim male advantage, authority and orthodoxies that represent men as 'natural leaders'.

Despite the fact that women predominate in terms of numbers of teachers, research commissioned by the NASUWT and undertaken by the University of Manchester confirms that it is men who are passported to early career success and rapid promotion.

Traditional orthodoxies have re-emerged in which teaching work has increasingly become monitored and externally regulated. This not only reflects the control of teachers' work, but the control of women as workers.

Since 2003, the NASUWT has been engaged in a social partnership with government and employers to enable teachers to reclaim their professionalism, to create greater fairness and equity in the operation of career development and promotional practices in schools and to ensure that statutory provisions relating to the schools workforce are enforced.

The aim of the agenda of social partnership working is to improve the working lives of teachers, the majority of whom are women.

There is still much more to be done. For example, to examine the factors that continue to impede career progress and to expose the detailed ways in which institutional sexism operates within our economy and our society. Some are evident – others less so as there has been very limited consideration of these issues.

There is a yawning chasm where hard, robust and detailed equalities data related to the school teacher workforce should be. The absence of such data means that women's experience of gender, ethnic and other forms of discrimination are silenced and denied. It is a national scandal that in a teaching workforce of well over half a million people, no robust data exists against which progress can be monitored and reviewed or by which the development of policy can be informed.

The trade union movement has a powerful and influential role to play. Much of the progress on equality issues has been either developed from within or campaigned for by trade unions and often by women within the movement.

Trade unions continue to be notable champions of equality and social justice. We have progressed from the days when, after the General Strike in 1926, the membership of trade unions was falling, the number of women working was increasing, and the trade unions wanted to limit the employment of women, who they felt were being employed at the expense of men. Yet at the same time they wanted to recruit women into membership to boost their numbers. To support this, the TUC launched a campaign to show that joining a trade union would lead to health and beauty!

The challenge for the trade union movement is to do more to champion gender equality at work and lead by example by doing so within its own ranks.

That is why we must be committed to creating the conditions that enable women's participation, to building networks of women within unions and to commissioning research to expose the way institutional sexism operates.

The equality duties introduced by the Government into public services have been welcome as they represent another step towards eliminating unlawful discrimination and to provide equality of opportunity but, although they are a useful lever for change, they will need to be strengthened. The Equality Bill now progressing through its parliamentary stages contains a number of essential provisions and is another stepping stone to equality.

Education has a critical role to play. Curriculum and career choices that boys and girls make are often founded on gender-based stereotypes that impact on later employment choices and earning potential. The structure of the curriculum, parental support and public attitudes are factors in transforming gender and cultural stereotypes.

We must address the scandalous squandering of talent that is taking place as a result of discrimination against women and girls. Waiting for market mechanisms and relying on the benevolence of a society run in the interests of men has, unsurprisingly, failed to deliver meaningful change.

All of us who believe in equality have a responsibility not to concede to doing what we have always done when the result is no significant progress on women's equality and women's rights. We need to look beyond traditional approaches and have the courage to continue the struggles of women like Emily Phipps and her sisters nearly a century ago for equal rights for all women.

Society will be all the better for it.

# Are Votes at Sixteen the Answer?
## by Emily Beardsmore

*Emily Beardsmore was until recently the Chair of the British Youth Council. At 23 she very much lives what she endorses, and has sat as a board member and company director on several other organizations. A passionate advocate for youth and student activism Emily is currently studying at University in London.*

**What are the next challenges** for democracy? Are "votes at 16" the answer? 80 years ago campaigners were celebrating because for the first time women had been given equal suffrage to men, through lowering the voting age for women from 30 to 21. Since then, the voting age has been lowered again to 18 in 1979, yet campaigns to lower the franchise age continue.

Many of the arguments used against lowering the voting age to 16 are similar to the ones used against extending the franchise to all young women, that young people are not mature enough, that they'll be unduly influenced by their peers or families or that young people are apathetic and don't really want the right to vote.

However it is this young generation who are the most informed that Britain has ever seen: they are the first to have access to an international network of friends and information through the internet; the first where Europe can be a day trip away; the first to have instant and 24 hour access to news; also the first to have gone through compulsory citizenship education in schools.

It is also this generation who will have to face up to the challenges of climate change, achieve equality for women, learn how to live in an increasingly globalised world and combat world poverty. We are the future leaders of this country and the world.

The role of online communications and social networking are changing the landscape of communications to something unrecognisable. The massive growth of social networking has changed how politicians can interact with constituents from Facebook to blogging to Twitter. These networks now demand almost instantaneous responses from politicians but also make them more accountable.

At no other point in history was it possible to know what your MP was doing most of the time just by the click of a mouse. New technologies are making it easier to connect with local and international politicians and are adding a new level of accountability to our society. As technology continues to develop and change we need to create a democracy that can continue to evolve and develop with new technologies; a democracy that will embrace new technology and move into the 21st century.

# A Great Act of Justice

A recent example of politicians powerfully using new technology was the election campaign of Barack Obama. This successfully mobilized the youth and student vote in unprecedented levels though a combination of online and grassroots methods.

These changes to society mean that changes to the political system need to happen to ensure that they are still relevant to future generations. We are living in a very different society than we were 80 years ago and democratic change seems to be lagging behind. This will mean that the way that we engage with democracy will need to change, young people are also the section of society most able to adapt to change and so we need to support them to be able to take charge of this change by lowering the voting age to 16.

So why does "votes at 16" matter so much now? Society has changed so much young people are increasingly asked to take more responsibility at an earlier age.

Young people have led the technology revolution and are the most likely to engage in new technology. They can be closer to politicians than any generation has been before. As new technologies develop and politicians engage more in them it will not only change the way we interact with democracy but the way future generations will engage with democracy.

In December 2008, 10,000 people turned out for the End Child Poverty march in London, and the majority of these marchers were young people. This is not surprising given that single issue campaigns are resonating more with young people, as well as the wider British public, than the dramas of party politics. This is how politics and democracy are changing, young people are very much engaged in global issues that impact locally and less on a national level.

Democracy needs to change to capture this spark of interest in issues: issues that are very much political, and have an impact on voting. Currently young people can be deprived of voting in a general election until they're 23, allowing votes at 16 would mean everyone would have the chance to vote by the time they turn 21. Research has shown that if young people vote the first time they are able to then they are more likely to continue voting for the rest of their lifetime. So by lowering the voting age it increases the chances that first time voters will be in an educational establishment and by having polling booths in schools, colleges and universities means that they are more likely to vote.

However this isn't just about passing a piece of legislation to lower the voting age. It's putting in place the infrastructure to support it. It is effective Local Youth Councils, showing young people that they can make a difference, it's improving the quality of citizenship education, it's helping young people who are a transient population to register to vote, its ensuring that polling stations are accessible to young people and it's encouraging politicians to go out there and talk to young people. If all these are implemented and young people have the right to vote at 16 then this will improve not only young peoples' engagement in politics but their engagement in society.

As I heard one MP say, whilst watching a debate on the issue in the House of Commons in June 2008, "There is no question of binge voting. It is a simple act, and it is not like the other behaviors that people are worried about. Young people cannot vote to excess or put themselves or others at risk by doing it".

Young peoples' engagement in politics beyond citizenship education and twitter feeds, could also be helped by knowing that they had a direct influence in choosing who represents them. In October 2008 there were elections where 16 and 17 years olds could vote in the British Isles in Jersey. In Austria where they recently lowered the voting age to 16, in the last local and regional elections the turnout was 75% of 16 and 17 year olds.

The reasons suggested for this significant turnout are that young people are able to act responsibly and to reflect their own beliefs, that young people make knowledge-based decisions, that young people are interested in politics and want to influence who governs them, and that young people take their rights and responsibilities seriously.

The campaign for votes at 16 will continue because it remains one of the most unjust realities in Britain today that 16 year olds are deemed adult enough to marry, have children, join the army and pay taxes. However, at 16 you can't vote for the politicians who set the laws on partnerships, send you to war or collect and spend your taxes. The campaign will continue until young people are valued as full members of society. It will continue because young people are demanding change. It will continue because until we lower the voting age we will continue to fail future generations of young people.

Democracy is about treating everyone as equals and ensuring that we take collective responsibility for the future of our country, this is why lowering the voting age to 16 will ensure the equal footing to engage everyone in the political process therefore increasing and enhancing democracy in Britain.

# Power Games: Examining the Barriers Holding Back Ethnic Minority Women
## by zohra moosa

*zohra moosa is currently Women's Rights Policy & Advocacy Officer at ActionAid. Prior to this role, zohra was Senior Policy & Campaigns Officer at the Fawcett Society where she ran Seeing Double, a national programme on the needs and priorities of ethnic minority women in the UK. Her publications include* Lifts and Ladders: resolving ethnic minority women's exclusion from power *and* Poverty Pathways: ethnic minority women's livelihoods. *She joined Fawcett from her role as Senior Policy Advisor to the Director of Strategy and Communications at the Commission for Racial Equality (CRE).*

**Ethnic minority women's** participation in politics is dramatically low. From Parliament right through to local councils, ethnic minority women are largely absent. With only two Black women MPs and ethnic minority women making up less than one percent of councillors, the extent of this gap is so severe that it amounts to a major power vacuum. Yet these positions represent some of the most powerful roles in British society, influencing decisions about resources and priorities that affect everyone in the country.

Extensive national and international work on women's representation, including that by the Fawcett Society, has contributed much to our understanding of the ongoing barriers facing women in politics.[14] Over the last three years, Fawcett's Seeing Double programme has been exposing how these barriers can be even higher for ethnic minority women in Britain.

A new report by Fawcett entitled *Lifts and Ladders: resolving ethnic minority women's exclusion from power* reveals that there are a number of very specific formal

---
[14] See for example *Women and politics: a briefing*, The Fawcett Society, June 2006.
[15] zohra moosa, *Lifts and Ladders: resolving ethnic minority women's exclusion from power*, The Fawcett Society, May 2009.

and informal rules operating in politics that are blocking ethnic minority women's access to power – rules that are artificial and unnecessary, and long overdue for a change.[15]

## The formal rules

Political institutions, including Parliament, local councils and even political parties, are formally structured in a way that makes it difficult for women to participate. Because of the disadvantages ethnic minority women also face because of racism, these 'rules' marginalise ethnic minority women even more severely.

For example, running for selection as a candidate for a political party currently requires attending evening meetings several nights a week, which makes it difficult for women with caring responsibilities to participate because of the lack of affordable and high quality childcare in the country. The childcare crunch is further compounded once women enter political office, especially when they become MPs. Parliament as an institution is designed as though MPs are men with no caring responsibilities, including by maintaining late hours most days of the week, with no recognition of the fact that care work is still unequally distributed between women and men.[16] In fact, while it continues to maintain a shooting gallery, Parliament provides no crèche facilities.[17]

This general childcare obstacle is particularly acute for some groups of ethnic minority women: research has found that Black women have the least access to free childcare, use childminders more than other groups, and pay for all or part of this minding at twice the rate of the next highest paying group.[18]

Running for selection as a political candidate also requires money to cover the costs of trips to constituencies, overnight accommodation if candidates do not live in the area, publicity and childcare or other caring responsibilities. These costs are borne by individual candidates, not political parties. As the gender pay gap for ethnic minority women means that they earn less than men and white women at all levels and across all sectors of employment, ethnic minority women are effectively disadvantaged in their ability to compete equally for political office.[19]

---

[16] http://www.parliament.uk/faq/business_faq_page.cfm, accessed on 25 March 2009.
[17] Oona King, *House Music: The Oona King Diaries*, Bloomsbury, 2007.
[18] Gary Craig, "Poverty among black and minority ethnic children" in Gabrielle Preston (ed) *At greatest risk: the children most likely to be poor*, Child Poverty Action Group, 2005.
[19] Lucinda Platt, *Pay gaps: the position of ethnic minority women and men*, Equal Opportunities Commission, 2006.
[20] Declan Hall and Rodney Brooke, *Members remuneration: Models, issues, incentives and barriers*, Councillors Commission, Department for Communities and Local Government, December 2007.
[21] *Routes to Power: Summary of discussion with ethnic minority women councillors*, The Fawcett Society, October 2007.

At the local level, the Government's Commission on Local Councillors has confirmed that the current system of remuneration discriminates against people because it is inconsistent between boroughs, treated as income for tax purposes which penalises women who receive benefits, and is often not adequate for the hours put into the role.[20] Fawcett's own research into the experiences of ethnic minority women councillors found becoming a councillor can actually cost some ethnic minority women money.[21]

## The informal rules

There are a number of informal 'rules' in politics that are highly exclusive. Many of them stem from and are enforced at the level of the political party, before permeating right through the rest of the political system.[22]

Political parties are voluntary organisations that operate as private membership-based clubs rather than professional bodies. They are not required to monitor or change their membership by any laws. Evidence has shown that as a result parties tend to recruit from a narrow section of society, with particularly poor representation from ethnic minorities.[23]

Once in, influence over a party relies on social connections and personal relationships. Personality has a huge influence on political success; it is fellow party members that select prospective political candidates to run for office. Potential candidates therefore have to demonstrate that they are loyal to party leaders and can 'get along' with other party members, most of whom are white men.

In selecting candidates, parties are not bound by any scrutiny and are not even required to monitor or report nominations; they are free to allow any biases to influence the process that they choose.[24] Work by the Centre for Women and Democracy has shown that party members tend to be highly risk averse, selecting candidates that mirror the ones that have won their seats in the past (namely white men) in the mistaken belief that the electorate will not vote in candidates that are too 'different'.[25]

Once in political office, politicians face many other exclusionary informal rules. In an interview with Fawcett, Dawn Butler MP revealed that she faced widespread

---

[22] Pippa Noris and Joni Lovenduski, *Political Recruitment: Gender, Race and Class in the British Parliament*, Cambridge University Press, 1995.

[23] Peter Riddell, *Candidate selection: The report of the commission on candidate selection*, Electoral Reform Society, September 2003.

[24] Rushanara Ali and Colm O'Cinneide, Our House? Race and representation in British politics, ippr, 2002.

[25] Submission to the Commission for Local Councillors, Centre for Women & Democracy, July 2007.

[26] 'Being different: My life as a Black woman MP. An interview with Dawn Butler MP', in zohra moosa (ed), Seeing Double: Race and gender in ethnic minority women's lives, pp 31-8, The Fawcett Society, March 2008.

racism and sexism in Parliament. Citing specific examples of unfair treatment, Dawn Butler was frank about the fact that her experiences were the result of being one of only two Black women MPs out of a House complement of 646.[26]

Fawcett's research with councillors has found similar challenges restrict ethnic minority women's access to positions at the local level.[27] Ethnic minority women councillors reported facing poor support and even discrimination from parties when attempting to become candidates.[28]

## Conclusion

Ethnic minority women are under-represented in politics in Britain because of the rules of the game. The formal and informal rules of political institutions in Britain, including Parliament, political parties and local councils, are actively blocking ethnic minority women from participating. Outdated government procedures create formal barriers, while exclusive cultures, especially within political parties, informally keep ethnic minority women out.

The longer Britain's democracy remains unrepresentative, the less entitled it is to its name: a democracy that is designed to keep some groups out can only ever be partial. Ethnic minority women's marginalisation from political power relative to their proportion of the population is stark and unjustifiable. In addition, as access to political power determines access to so many other rights, addressing these obstacles to ethnic minority women's representation is a matter of significant import.

The suffrage movement evolved out of the abolitionist movement.[29] Yet almost a hundred years after the Franchise Act and two hundred since the abolition of trans-Atlantic slavery, both causes remain incomplete while ethnic minority women continue to struggle for equal political power. The lead-up to the next election offers the chance to take bold steps towards the full emancipation of ethnic minority women.

---

[27] Routes to Power: Summary of discussion with ethnic minority women councillors, The Fawcett Society, October 2007.
[28] See also Representing the future: The report of the Councillors Commission, Councillors Commission, Department for Communities and Local Government, December 2007.
[29] Kimberly McKee, 'The hidden roots of feminism', StopGap, p. 12, The Fawcett Society, Spring 2007.

# Making politics work for women: changing the way we vote
## by Beatrice Barleon

*Beatrice Barleon was until recently the Women's Officer at the Electoral Reform Society where she was responsible for the overall strategy of the women's campaign. Since her arrival at the Society in 2007 she was, amongst other things, instrumental in setting up the Women and the Vote campaign. Before coming to the Society Beatrice had worked in a number of other campaigning organisations and as a researcher in television, and now works in a senior role for a prominent mental health charity.*

**Women in the UK** are still severely under-represented in politics 80 years on since the first election took place under universal suffrage rules. This is a fact and something that needs to change. Parties have tried and continue to try to improve the diversity of their candidates and get them elected; however, we are still nowhere near achieving anything resembling equal representation. The reason for this is that there are a number of structural barriers in the way of greater diversity in politics and in the way of a more diverse range of voices being heard. Unless we address these obstacles, equal representation will continue to remain a goal rather than become reality.

This article looks at one of these barriers and the impact it has on the number of women making it into national politics – our First-Past-the-Post (FPTP) electoral system. Unfortunately, changing the way we vote for our representatives is often sidelined in discussions about what causes and cures there are to improving the diversity of our Parliament. This, however, is most likely to do with the fact that turkeys just don't like to vote for Christmas and that promises of change tend to be revoked once an election is won. But there is also another reason. Despite the fact that some people, like the Australian academic Marian Sawer, understand FPTP to be 'a form of indirect discrimination against women in public life', the relationship between the way we vote for our representatives and the under-representation of women is not direct in the sense that if you change the system, you automatically get more women. If things were that easy, we would have done it a long time ago. Structural change is inevitably complex and requires action on many levels, which means that the link is more subtle, but nevertheless important.

The biggest issue with the First-Past-the-Post system used to elect our MPs is that it inhibits change and reinforces the status quo. Given that FPTP was developed during a patriarchal empire and ultimately reflects a time when the male head of the household was deemed to be able to speak for all under him, this is deeply problematic. Had the history of the UK have been one of a matriarchal society – where only the female heir could inherit and we had only one male Prime Minister – then we would today most likely be bemoaning the lack of men in politics. So, while the system is not inherently sexist in itself, history has come to mean that it indirectly discriminates against those previously excluded from political life.

Under FPTP voters only have limited opportunity to dislodge a significant number of male MPs in the House of Commons at any single General Election, for the obvious reason that many represent constituencies where their party has a comfortable majority. These men in effect therefore enjoy a monopoly status since they normally only 'lose' their seat when they choose to stand down or are de-selected. Only rarely, normally during times of epic political shifts, such as during the 1997 elections, is it the case that they may become replaced by a female candidate from the opposition party. Nicholas Budgen, for example, had survived six General Elections before Jenny Jones managed to oust him in 1997. This effect is greatly retarding the chances of reaching gender parity in the next 20 years, since it severely restricts the number of vacancies. The more openings there are for new people to enter formal politics, the more opportunities there are also for women and for parties to take steps to ensure that more women are elected.

But that's not all. Politics under FPTP determines that parties need an almost gravity-defying amount of political will to succeed with gender equality when they only get to chose one candidate per constituency and when the amount of constituencies they actually have any chance of winning has been further curtailed by the electoral map that First-Past-the-Post creates. While there is no doubt that all of the parties have made significant efforts to improve the situation for women over the last ten years, it is still an unfortunate reality that around thirty percent of seats in the most recent General Elections continue to be male only contests, with women often clustering in the same constituencies.[30] The prevailing image of a politician is still one of a white-middle class male, and the way we vote does little to challenge that.

---

[30] Harrison, Lisa (2005) Electoral Strategies and Female Candidacy: Comparing Trends in the 2005 and 2001 General Elections, Paper presented to the Elections, Parties and Public Opinion Specialist Group Annual Conference

However, the reason our voting system is considered to be one of the least favourable in terms of improving female political representation doesn't just lie in its mechanics but also in the type of politics it creates. Majoritarian systems are almost famous for the confrontational political culture they encourage. This is not only off-putting to voters more generally, and therefore clearly affects the number and variety of people wanting to become involved in politics, but if the Equal Opportunities Commission, now the EHRC, is to be believed then it disproportionately discourages women from standing as candidates. And without more female candidates we will never achieve the goal of equal representation.

So what can we do about all this? While changing the way we vote alone to a more proportional system will not be enough to guarantee equality in representation, it would go a long way to ensuring not only that more women will be gracing the green benches in Westminster in the future, but also that female voices will be heard more strongly. It would not only help create better and more opportunities for women, but also alter the type of politics in which they operate. Proportional representation systems are better placed to accommodate the heterogeneity of votes and perspectives present within British society. Which electoral system a society chooses to filter votes into seats and political power speaks volumes about the nature of politics in that society.

Clearly, the extent to which parties capitalise on the greater opportunities such a system would offer depend on the degree of political will and a parallel commitment to removing other social and cultural barriers to women's advancement in political life. However, in the words of Luta Shaba, 'only through proportional representation can women, together with other previously marginalised groups, rise'.

# A Brief Snip of Time
## by Boni Sones

*Boni Sones OBE is author of "Women in Parliament: The New Suffragettes", with Professor Joni Lovenduski and Margaret Moran MP, published by Politico's. She has been a political journalist covering social affairs issues in print, radio and TV for 30 years. In January 09 she was awarded an OBE for "Services to Broadcasting and PR". She is currently Executive Producer of Women's Parliamentary Radio*

**The date is Tuesday** 17th March 2009. I am privileged to be sitting at a Government Equalities Office event listening to ministers talking about their forthcoming Equality Bill. It is, the Solicitor General, Vera Baird QC MP tells us, "some of the most pioneering legislation in the World" on equality. She then takes us, the audience, including some of us "oldies" through a trip down our own memory lane summarising what Labour governments have done over the past 40 years to further the equality agenda, protect human rights and to tackle discrimination.

Now it is all to be consolidated in one new Equality Bill. It will bring together the existing separate duties covering race, disability and gender and extend it to cover pregnancy and maternity, age, sexual orientation, religion, belief and gender reassignment in a new, strengthened public sector duty. It, will she says, "clarify, strengthen, and broaden existing laws" and offer the same "fair opportunities in life" to all. The mechanism to deliver this will be public sector procurement policies.

Ms Baird reminds us of the importance of the representation of women in Parliament and that as a result of positive discrimination and the All Women Shortlists that Labour introduced the number of women MPs has risen from 9 per cent in 1997 to just under 20 per cent now. The law will be extended to allow political parties to use All Women Shortlists at least until 2030.

It's Harriet Harman's QC MP the Minister for Women and Equality's turn next. Again, like Ms Baird, we run from the past to the present and a few of those shocker statistics are lobbed in. "The pay gap in the financial services industry is still 44 per cent"; that Ms Harman tells us show the markets have "failed" and that fairness and diversity doesn't just happen of its own accord, it needs a considerable push and a legislative lead.

Ms Harman is particularly good and her words have real passion when she gets onto the topic of the so called "old boys' network". "Economies that prosper don't have the stagnation that an old boys' network creates," says Ms Harman.

Let's just declare at this stage, that the introduction of the Equality Bill is being supported by all parties, Conservatives and Liberal Democrats too, in fact they keep urging the government to "bring it on" sooner rather than later. The Conservative women Theresa May, MP, the Shadow Secretary of State for Work and Pensions and Shadow Minister for Women, Caroline Spelman MP, the Shadow Secretary of State for Communities and Local Government, and Eleanor Laing MP, Shadow Minister for Justice, have with others, been reforming their own party structures to improve the representation of women and ethnic minorities through the extremely ably run "Women2Win" campaign.

The Liberal Democrats have an equal smattering of equality minded women including Lynne Featherstone MP, Shadow Equalities Minister, Jo Swinson MP, Shadow Minister for Foreign Affairs, and Sandra Gidley MP Shadow health spokesperson.

Four years after authoring the book "Women in Parliament: The New Suffragettes" with Margaret Moran MP and Professor Joni Lovenduski I can still get an energy from turning up in a room and listening to these speeches. This is odd, my attention spans are not renowned for being long.

Making what can be a slightly dry, worthy topic, "live" is not easy. The media too often ridicules their efforts, and ridicules them, whether it is Ms May for her shoes or low cut top, or Ms Harman for even thinking she might be leader of her party one day!!

On behalf of my fellow journalists – a profession I have always been proud to be part of – I too wanted to offer an apology to Ms Harman and any other women MP who has been defined by their clothing rather than their policies or words. It is often, pure misogyny that women MPs find themselves on the receiving end of through the poisonous copy of others.

What this group of women MPs are doing across parties might seem somewhat limp compared to the protests, rallies, fire bombs, imprisonment, and even death of one suffragette, Emily Wilding Davison, to win the right for women to vote 91 years ago, but there is clearly a time-line running from those days to now…. Tuesday 17th March 2009.

80 years since the first General Election with universal suffrage in the UK there is a real life equalities agenda being pursued by government, and an Equalities Minister, Maria Eagle, MP. That equalities agenda extends across party, and worthy, "terms

like public sector procurement policies" and "pay audits" are used universally by all now. It is not the "what if" but the "how" of equality that is now being pursued.

Were these issues of their time? Would there have been an Equality Bill without the Labour women of '97 there to promote and lobby for it? To answer this I would have to quote from Ms Harman herself who is fond of telling the story of how when meetings are called on any so called "women's issue" it's the "women who turn up". This I believe to be true having witnessed it for many years myself. Their list of championing social progress includes issues such as domestic violence, child trafficking, prostitution, the pay gap, forced marriages, tax credits, and even removing VAT on sanitary ware.

When academics attempt to measure the impact on social issues of women in Parliaments they resort to technical terms which in my view cloud the issues. In attempting to measure progress they clearly neglect the huge and significant emotional difference that having a group of women across party in a workplace can make; or to use Ms Harman's terms – "the old boys' network" is fractured.

There is one thing most women MPs are agreed on and that is the House of Commons in 1997, before 121 women got elected to Westminster, the largest number ever, was an old boys' network like no other. That change came about because as a result of All Women Shortlists through which Labour got 101 of its women MPs elected.

A swing against the Labour party will disproportionately lead to Labour women losing their seats at the next general election, but if Ms May is right, then with the Conservative women waiting to break through in so called safe seats the House of Commons may see women's representation staying much as it is.

This isn't good enough. Enter the Solicitor General Vera Baird again and her speech on Tuesday 17th March 2009. On current progress, she says, it will not be your children, your grandchildren, or even your great-grandchildren, but your great-great-great-great-grandchildren—at the earliest—who may see a House of Commons with equal numbers of men and women.

You can write any date you want into the history books. There have been 20 General Elections since the flapper election of 30 May 1929. Sitting listening to these speeches on Tuesday 17th March 2009, the passion, tenacity, stamina, and guile needed for a fight is sill there. Or as Ms Harman bravely told us "a row can sometimes be a good performance indicator". Indeed Ms Harman it is.

A row over the new Equality Bill, 80 years since women first voted in a General Election is a very good thing indeed. Where's the stone, I want to chuck it at the window….no… I have to temper my anger and read up on public sector procurement policies instead. Bring on that "row" Ms Harman for all our sakes.

# And Finally ...

The next general election will be the twenty-fifth to be held since any women could vote or enter parliament, and the twenty-first since all women could vote on an equal basis with men.

Since that time, much progress has been made. Women now constitute nearly 20% of the House of Commons, and have held almost all the major offices of state. They have been admitted to the House of Lords as both life and hereditary peers, and have served as ministers in almost all departments of government. Yet they are still in a minority, and the general perception of what a politician is is still white, male and middle-aged. When will more progress be made?

Prognostications made on all sides are generally fairly gloomy. Yet there are grounds for real optimism. For the first time all of the political parties have working strategies for increasing the number of women MPs they have, and the next general election will tell how successful these have been. There may be a general disenchantment with politics, yet young women who believe that the world needs to be changed, and that they are just the people to do it, are still emerging. Women politicians are still ridiculed and insulted by the media, yet they show no sign of giving in and slinking back to more traditional backroom roles.

Moreover, other changes are on the horizon. More BME women than ever before will be in the next House of Commons, and in all likelihood more will be in senior roles. There will be more women of all backgrounds on the backbenches of all the main parties, and the House of Commons will again 'look different' from before.

And yet ... the actual overall percentage of women MPs is unlikely to rise by very much; those that there are are just going to be spread a little more equally across the House. Women will still have to juggle one of the most stressful, intrusive and high profile jobs there are with domestic responsibilities, and some will still find this too onerous. Women in powerful roles will still be belittled and demeaned by a media style that seems to see all women in terms of what they wear, and women who campaign for more equality, or who venture to describe themselves as feminists, will still be subjected to what are sometimes astonishing, if not disturbing, outpourings of bile.

In fact, the next general election will be a watershed for women's representation. There are some scenarios in which it could actually go backwards, and several in which it could stand still. If either of these things happens, or if any increase in the number of women MPs is negligible, all three of the political parties will need to ask themselves some serious questions. Just how committed are they to equality of representation? Do they really believe that women have a wealth of expertise, skill and experience to bring to the political table, or do they just trot this out as rhetoric when necessary? And, if they accept that more than half of the population should be more visible in the legislature, what steps are they going to take to make it happen?

Almost all of the countries which have done well in terms of women's representation have employed quota systems in one form or another. Here, the Labour Party has gone down that route with their all-women shortlists, and these have certainly been highly successful in delivering significant numbers of women in parliament. But both the Conservative and the Liberal Democrat Parties have developed alternative ways of making progress, and these would be well worth examining in some depth, particularly if they make a real difference. If the UK can find an accommodation between compulsion and encouragement, and if that can be applied to all parties so as to increase the speed of change, then the Mother of Parliaments might again be leading the world.

Recent events have led people of all persuasions to believe that Britain's democratic system needs real change. Changing the way politics works as well as the way it looks is one of the keys to re-engaging a jaded public interest in how a democratic society should govern itself. As contributors to this volume have suggested, there are all sorts of things that could be done to make a difference – but there needs to be some coherence about whatever strategy is adopted, and the eventual outcome needs to reflect the way in which society itself has changed over the last eighty years since the first 'irresponsible' women in their twenties went to vote.

Women born in 1910 acquired, as their lives went on, rights which their mothers and grandmothers scarcely imagined. But the new millennium presents its own challenges as the nature of democracy changes, and as society's perception of what democracy should mean continues to develop from simple voting for representatives to more complex forms of participation.

When Ellen Wilkinson described the 1928 Representation of the People (Equal Franchise) Act as 'a great act of justice' she saw it as the end of the journey. But as this book has demonstrated, it was in fact just a staging post. What the suffragettes, suffragists and pioneering women parliamentarians began in the twentieth century still awaits completion in the twenty-first.

# Sources and Acknowledgements

## PHOTOGRAPHS

Cover: Photographs of Margaret Bondfield, Jennie Lee, Megan Lloyd George, and Ellen Wilkinson all © National Portrait Gallery, London. Photo of Nancy Astor © Topical Press Agency/Hulton Archives/Getty Images

Photographs of Nancy Astor (P21), Margaret Wintringham (P22), Katharine Stewart-Murray, Duchess of Atholl (P35), Vera, Lady Terrington (P46), Labour Women MPs in 1929 (P50), Barbara Castle (P78), Alice Bacon (P79), Eveline Hill (P83), Edith Pitt (P84), Shirley Williams (P92), Margaret Thatcher (P104) all © National Portrait Gallery, London

Photograph of Mo Mowlam (P105) © Victoria Carew Hunt / National Portrait Gallery, London

Photograph of Constance Markiewicz (p20) © Keogh/Hulton Archive/Getty Images

Photographs of Eleanor Rathbone (P70) and Bessie Braddock (P77) © Hulton Archive/Getty Images

## SOURCES

**Hansard : HC Deb 29 March 1928 vol 215 cc1359-481** – all quotations from the 1928 debate on the Representation of the People (Equal Franchise) Bill are taken from the online Hansard archive at http://hansard.millbanksystems.com/commons/1928/mar/29/representation-of-the-people-equal#S5CV0215P0_19280329_HOC_344

**Centre for the Advancement of Women in Politics** at Queens University Observatory at www.qub.ac.uk/cawp/observatory – main source for details of which women were elected at which elections.

**Oxford Dictionary of National Biography** (online edition) – this invaluable resource has been the principal source for information about individual women.

**Women In Parliament & Government** – House of Commons Library, SN/SG/1250, 30 June 2009

**BBC Radio 4 Woman's Hour Timeline** – excellent for background information and 'firsts'

**Notes on election work: for the use of women candidates and their workers**, with a foreword by Viscountess Astor. NUSEC, 1921, held in the Brotherton Special Collection at the University of Leeds

**Phillips, Marion; The organisation of women within the Labour Party: a handbook for officers and members of women's sections**, by Marion Philips, published by the Labour Party, 1921, and with an introduction by Arthur Henderson

**Law, Cheryl; Suffrage and Power: the Women's Movement 1918-1928**, IBTauris & Co., London, 2000 – Excellent and informative account of the wider women's movement between the first and second Enfranchisement Acts.

**Sones, Boni, (with Margaret Moran and Joni Lovenduski) ; Women in Parliament: The New Suffragettes**, Politicos Publishing, London, 2005 – Splendid account of the experiences of women in parliament in the late twentieth century, and, in particular, of the record 1997 intake.

**Times House of Commons 1929 and 1931**, Politicos Publishing, 2003

**Useful websites** have included those for all three of the main political parties and their relevant women's organisations and groups, as well as more general sites:

| | |
|---|---|
| Conservative Women's Organisation: | www.conservativewomen.org.uk |
| Conservative Party | www.conservatives.com |
| Women2Win | www.women2win.com |
| Labour Party | www.labour.org.uk |
| Labour Women's Network | www.lwn.org.uk |
| Liberal Democrats | www.libdems.org.uk |
| Women Liberal Democrats | www.womenlibdems.org.uk |
| Campaign for Gender Balance | www.genderbalance.org.uk |
| UK Political Information & Electoral Data | www.ukpolitical.info |
| International Parliamentary Union | www.ipu.org |
| Liberal Democrat History Group | www.liberalhistory.org.uk |
| National Archives | www.nationalarchives.gov.uk |
| Quota Database | www.quotaproject.org |
| Women's Library | www.londonmet.ac.uk/thewomenslibrary |
| Houses of Parliament | www.parliament.uk |
| European Parliament | www.europarl.europa.eu |
| Scottish Parliament | www.scottish.parliament.uk |
| Welsh Assembly | www.assemblywales.org |

# Index

**Abbott**, Diane 13, 99, 101, 106, 113, 124
**Adamson**, Jennie 69, 73, 75, 118
**Amos**, Valerie 13, 119, 123, 138
**Applin**, Colonel 40, 41
**Armstrong**, Hilary 101, 113, 119, 121, 124
**Astor**, Nancy 7, 10, 13, 18, 19, 21, 22, 23, 31, 32, 39, 41, 43, 48, 49, 66, 67, 69, 72, 130, 133
**Atholl**, Duchess of 18, 19, 31, 32, 35, 41, 48, 49, 66, 67, 118, 130
**Bacon**, Alice 74, 75, 79, 81, 86
**Baldwin**, Stanley 9, 11, 31, 32, 33, 37, 39, 43, 44, 48
**Beckett**, Margaret 13, 88, 89, 94, 101, 113, 119, 121, 123, 124, 138
**Bentham**, Ethel 49, 50, 52, 55
**Blears**, Hazel 113, 119, 122, 124
**Bondfield**, Margaret 13, 18, 19, 31, 41, 42, 49, 50, 51, 67, 118, 135
**Boothroyd**, Betty 11, 13, 88, 89, 91, 108, 113
**Bottomley**, Virginia 101, 113, 119, 120, 124
**Braddock**, Bessie 74, 75, 77, 81, 86
**Butler**, Dawn 13, 106, 119, 124, 180, 181
**Castle**, Barbara 74, 75, 78, 80, 81, 85, 86, 88, 89, 118-120
**Cazalet**, Thelma 52, 69, 118
**Cockerill**, Sir George 39
**Conservative Party** 31, 32, 36, 38, 42, 48, 50, 66, 80, 83, 84, 91, 96, 104, 130, 131, 133, 186
**Conservative Women's Organization** 131
**Cooper**, Yvette 114, 119, 122, 125
**Dalton**, Ruth 18, 19
**Devlin**, Bernadette 30, 85, 86, 89, 93
**Dunwoody**, Gwynneth 86, 88, 89, 101, 109, 114, 125
**Eagle**, Angela 13, 112, 114, 124
**Eagle**, Maria 114, 125, 137, 186
**Ewing**, Winifred 85, 86, 89
**Ford**, Patricia 80, 81
**Guinness**, Gwendoline see Iveagh, Countess of
**Hamilton**, Mary Agnes 49, 50, 57
**Harman**, Harriet 101, 114, 119, 121, 126, 185-187
**Hart**, Judith 86, 90, 101, 118, 120
**Herbison**, Margaret 75, 81, 86, 118
**Hewitt**, Patricia 115, 119, 121, 126
**Horsburgh**, Florence 69, 73, 82, 118, 120, 130
**Iveagh**, Countess of 18, 19, 36, 40-42, 48, 49, 65, 69, 130
**Jewson**, Dorothy 13, 18, 19, 31, 60, 135
**Jowell**, Tessa 115, 119, 121, 126
**Joynson-Hicks**, William 15, 37, 38, 39, 130
**Kelly**, Ruth 115, 119, 122, 126
**Labour Party** 18, 31, 32, 34, 37, 38, 48, 50, 51, 53, 54, 55, 66, 67, 72, 73, 77, 79, 88, 92, 94, 96, 97, 99, 110, 112, 123, 135, 136, 145, 155, 156, 185, 187, 189
**Labour Women's Network** 135
**Lawrence**, Susan 13, 18, 19, 31, 34, 41, 49, 50, 118, 135
**Lee**, Jennie 48, 49, 50, 53, 74, 75, 82, 86
**Liberal Democrats** 99, 107, 123, 134, 141, 142, 189
**Liberal Party** 18, 37, 38, 48, 50, 54, 66, 88, 99, 141,
**Lloyd George**, David 48, 54
**Lloyd George**, Megan 49, 54, 66, 67, 69, 75, 80, 82, 85, 86, 107, 141, 154
**Lucas-Tooth**, Sir Hugh 47
**MacArthur**, Mary 17, 51
**Macdonald**, Margo 18, 90
**Macdonald**, Ramsay 32, 34, 50, 52, 54
**Manning**, Leah 52, 69, 75
**Markiewicz**, Constance 13, 17, 18, 20
**McLaughlin**, Patricia 80, 82
**Michie**, Ray 67, 99, 102, 107, 116, 141
**Morris**, Estelle 116, 119, 121, 127
**Mosley**, Cynthia 49, 50, 72
**Philipson**, Mabel 18, 19, 31, 41, 45, 10
**Phillips**, Marion 49, 50, 55, 67, 135
**Phipps**, Emily 7, 171, 173
**Picton-Turberville**, Edith 49, 50, 56
**Private Member's Bills** 31, 32, 37
**Qualification of Women Act 1918** 17
**Rathbone**, Eleanor 13, 30, 35, 49, 66, 67, 70, 73, 74, 75, 147
**Representation of the People (Equal Franchise) Act (1918)** 16, 139
**Representation of the People (Equal Franchise) Bill/Act (1928)** 10, 11, 33, 36, 37-44, 189
**Representation of the People Act (1969)** 85
**Runciman**, Hilda 18, 19, 61, 141
**Scotland**, Patricia 13, 112
**Shepherd**, Gillian 102, 117, 119, 120, 128
**Short**, Clare 102, 117, 119, 121, 128
**Sinn Fein** 18, 19, 20, 93, 147, 152, 162, 164, 165
**Smith**, Jacqui 13, 117, 122, 123, 128, 138
**Snowden**, Philip 39, 43
**Speaker's Conference (promised)** 32, 37, 54
**Speaker's Conference 1916** 16, 139
**Speaker's Conference 2009** 10, 136, 143, 144, 168
**Stewart-Murray**, Katharine see Atholl, Duchess of
**Summerskill**, Edith 69, 73, 76, 82, 118
**Summerskill**, Shirley 85, 87, 90
**Taylor**, Ann 13, 90, 103, 117, 119, 120, 129, 138
**Terrington**, Vera 18, 19, 24, 31, 46, 141
**Thatcher**, Margaret 10, 13, 80, 87, 88, 90, 92, 96, 97, 103, 104, 109, 110, 118-120, 131
**The 300 Club** 99
**Wilkinson**, Ellen 3, 9, 19, 31, 35, 40, 41, 49, 50, 67, 69, 71, 73, 74, 76, 118, 120, 189
**Williams**, Shirley 85, 87, 89, 92, 99, 103, 119, 120, 141
**Wintringham**, Margaret 13, 18, 19, 22, 31, 63, 141
**Women's Liberal Federation** 22, 66, 141
**Women's Labour League** 52, 66, 135
**Women's Party** 18, 147
**Women2Win** 131, 134, 186